The BALLS.IE
Guide to Life

ABOUT BALLS.IE

Balls.ie is an Irish sports website founded in 2010 by Donny Mahoney, Brian Reynolds and Ger Gilroy. Since then, it has become an essential destination for news, gossip and sideways analysis of the wonderful world of Irish sport and beyond. Among the highlights of the site's existence are being threatened with a lawsuit by Bayern Munich's Mario Götze after publishing a photo of him in Speedos with his manhood apparently at half-mast, and being called 'a reputable website' by Joe Duffy on *Liveline*.

The Balls Media family grew this year to include theslicedpan.com. Sure, self-praise is no praise, but we believe we provide the best and funniest coverage of Irish life online. Tell your friends and cousins.

Mark, Brian, Conor, PJ and Barry: a Balls.ie five-a-side selection, July 2015.

The BALLS.IE

Guide to Life

THE O'BRIEN PRESS
DUBLIN

First published 2015 by The O'Brien Press Ltd,
12 Terenure Road East, Rathgar, Dublin 6, D06 HD27, Ireland.
Tel: +353 1 4923333; Fax: +353 1 4922777
E-mail: books@obrien.ie
Website: www.obrien.ie

ISBN: 978-1-84717-785-8

Conceived by Donny Mahoney and Brian Reynolds
Compiled by Donny Mahoney
Written by Donny Mahoney, Conor Neville, PJ Browne, Mark Farrelly,
Conor O'Leary, John Owens, Brian Reynolds, Paul Ring and Mikey Traynor

Our thanks to sports photography agency Sportsfile (sportsfile.com)
for the use of archive photographs throughout this book.

Thanks also to Barry Downes for the illustrations on pp. 39–40, 46–51, 67,
94–95 and 98–100.

10 9 8 7 6 5 4 3 2 1
20 19 18 17 16 15

Printed and bound in the Czech Republic by Finidr Ltd.

The paper in this book is produced using pulp from managed forests.

FOREWORD

First of all, we lied to you. If you bought this book expecting advice on how to drive a tractor, attain mindfulness or plan your pension, you're in the wrong place.

This is a *kind* of guide though. Since 2010, Balls.ie has been trawling the internet, listening to the beating heart of the Irish sports fan. Oh, the things we've seen! Two million jokes have been made about Robbie Keane playing for his boyhood club, Irish soccer fans took over Poland for two weeks, Johnny Maher got angry, Brian O'Driscoll retired, Conor McGregor happened, a documentary was even made about John Delaney ...

Along the way, there's been a lot of eejitry and a few genuinely life-changing moments. Think back to the desolation when Ryan Crotty scored that try for the All-Blacks in the corner of the Aviva in November 2013. Or the ecstasy when Nigel Owens blew the final whistle on the 2015 Six Nations with England encamped on the French try line. Balls.ie was there, in real time, compiling all of these memorable moments. We've learned a few things about Irish sports fans along the way. In a sense, this book is a loose attempt to mark the trajectory of the modern Irish sports fan, from his birth around Euro '88 and Italia '90, through the disillusioned Michelle Smith years, into the heady days of the Celtic Tiger and the horrible hangover that followed, arriving in whatever era we find ourselves in now.

It's our belief that many of the silliest and most important moments in Irish life have happened on the sports pitch. This is our attempt to document them.

Donny Mahoney,
Co-founder, Balls.ie

Contents

26

42

BALLS OF FUN PAGES!

How to Streak Like an IRISHMAN

Perhaps because of our miserable climate and Catholic indoctrination, the Irish male has always had a rather unusual relationship with his body. Unlike his tanned, lithe, Speedo-sporting continental cousins, he is often simultaneously delighted and disgusted with the sight of himself in the nip.

Yet there's nothing quite like the floodlit, beer-soaked atmosphere of the live sporting event to induce the Irish sports fan to nudity. Suddenly, with the world watching, all shame is gone. Clothes are shucked off, expensive match tickets are forsaken, arrest is risked and public humiliation is all but assured. Why? The thrill of ultimate eejitry must partly explain it. And streaking is perhaps the greatest act of protest for the sports-loving Irish male. It's a bold, anti-establishment action that doesn't rock the boat in the slightest. Slightly brave, mostly stupid: that's the streaker in a nutshell.

THE SCHOOLS STREAKER

The compulsion to traipse nude across the playing field is strongest in the young. Witness these upstanding chaps exposing themselves at Leinster Cup games in 2004 (left) and 2006 (right). Schools-rugby streaking seems to be one of the many exuberances that came into vogue during the Celtic Tiger. The shortage of stewards at these games would have given these fellows a clear path across the pitch; no doubt their headmasters took note though.

THE SUCCESSFUL STREAKER

Look, you don't take to the field in your jocks to be tackled a couple of seconds later by some bolshie steward. Streaking is a fleeting opportunity to momentarily live an entire sports career – the thrill of the chase, the roar of the crowd, the knowledge that thousands of people have their eyes on you. This patriot at a 2002 Six Nations game between Ireland and Italy may have forgotten his shoes, but he came ready to play.

THE NEEDY STREAKER

As if pausing a frenetic hurling match in full flow isn't criminal enough, some streakers are occasionally inspired to embrace their sporting heroes too. Somehow, at the Leinster hurling final of 2006, Wexford's Declan Ruth resisted the urge to bludgeon this lad in the black underwear. Most would have forgiven him.

THE BLASPHEMOUS STREAKER

Everyone who sets out on this bare-skinned voyage, you must presume, does it with a higher purpose in mind. This streaker at a Shannon–St Mary's AIL game in 2000 took to the pitch to remind players and spectators alike that we all have our crosses to bear.

THE BRANDCENTRIC STREAKER

The majority of streakers to grace Croker's hallowed turf are Dubs – it's a way of staking their claim on the place. Examine this fine specimen who made himself known to GAA fans at the Dublin–Donegal All-Ireland quarter-final replay back in August 2002. So concerned was he that everyone recognise him as a Jackeen that he placed the Arnotts logo across his bare chest. The rest of the paint job we can't quite vouch for, but we do respect his early noughties half Johnny Rotten/ half Mark Vaughan cyberpunk hairstyle that's sadly gone out of fashion amongst both Dublin footballers and fans.

THE DO-GOODER STREAKER

You might hate streakers, but what about those who bare all for a just cause? Can public nudity intended to advertise worthy causes for the betterment and health of mankind be sanctioned? That answer is still no, but we do commend these chaps' efforts.

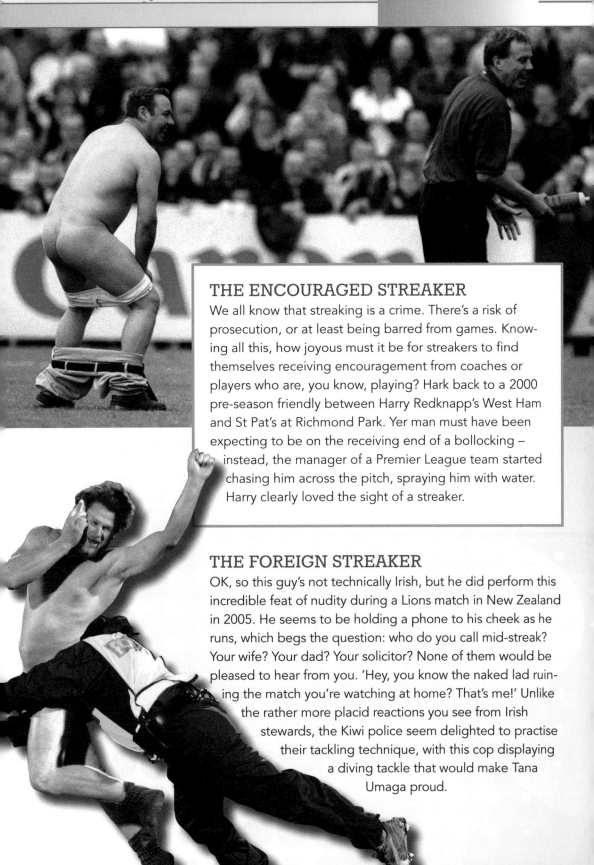

THE ENCOURAGED STREAKER

We all know that streaking is a crime. There's a risk of prosecution, or at least being barred from games. Knowing all this, how joyous must it be for streakers to find themselves receiving encouragement from coaches or players who are, you know, playing? Hark back to a 2000 pre-season friendly between Harry Redknapp's West Ham and St Pat's at Richmond Park. Yer man must have been expecting to be on the receiving end of a bollocking – instead, the manager of a Premier League team started chasing him across the pitch, spraying him with water. Harry clearly loved the sight of a streaker.

THE FOREIGN STREAKER

OK, so this guy's not technically Irish, but he did perform this incredible feat of nudity during a Lions match in New Zealand in 2005. He seems to be holding a phone to his cheek as he runs, which begs the question: who do you call mid-streak? Your wife? Your dad? Your solicitor? None of them would be pleased to hear from you. 'Hey, you know the naked lad ruining the match you're watching at home? That's me!' Unlike the rather more placid reactions you see from Irish stewards, the Kiwi police seem delighted to practise their tackling technique, with this cop displaying a diving tackle that would make Tana Umaga proud.

How to Become the Ultimate Irish Sports Fan

The soul of the Irish sports supporter is a beautiful thing, but it needs to be refined and protected. The ultimate sports fan is faithful and loyal, determined and unafraid to voice his (very specific) opinions. Here is our step-by-step guide to being the best you can be.

GET BLOCKED BY STEPHEN JONES ON TWITTER

Getting blacklisted by *The Sunday Times*'s pre-eminent rugby crank for, say, shamelessly celebrating the relative greatness of Peter O'Mahony over Dan Lydiate is a huge milestone in Irish sports fandom. Just be prepared to be called a 'twerp' spouting 'drivel' and abused for your lack of followers. Jones's Twitter account is protected (largely thanks to Irish rugby fans), so you will have to earn his trust first. Express some nostalgia for the '05 Welsh Grand Slam team and you should be fine.

REMIND MAYO PEOPLE THEY HAVEN'T WON AN ALL-IRELAND IN AGES ...

... irrespective of how shite your own county is. A cruel one, yes, but something most sports fans from the other thirty-one counties will admit to. Even if you come from a county that has never won anything or is unlikely to ever win anything, you can still engage in this activity. Until such time as Mayo win the big one, this game will be allowed to go on and on.

CONTINUE TO MAKE IRONIC REFERENCES TO GARY BREEN'S LEGENDARY STATUS

Memorise the words of the terrace classic 'We All Dream of a Team of Gary Breens' (sung to the tune of 'Yellow Submarine'). It is not an onerous task. Whenever asked to instance a legendary Irish footballer from the late-'90s, always blurt out Breen's name first.

WHENEVER POSSIBLE, TALK ABOUT ROY KEANE

In the past 150 years, there have been five major figures in Irish life: Charles Stewart Parnell, Michael Collins, Éamon de Valera, Charlie Haughey and Roy Keane. All five inspired fanatical love and fanatical hatred in equal measure among their countrymen. At this stage, there should be a Keano Studies department at UCC.

APPOINT YOURSELF AS A HURLING AMBASSADOR

We've all seen the confused tourists in the pub on an August Sunday afternoon, trying to wrap their heads around the spectacle on the telly. It is your patriotic duty to explain what's going on. Don't worry about over-hyping; such a thing is impossible. If there was a Nobel Prize for Sport, the first ten prizes would go to hurlers – if not to the sport itself. Tell them that not only is hurling the fastest game on grass, it is the best game in the world. This is not hyperbole, just a sober statement of fact.

BLAME ALL OUR WOES ON JOHN DELANEY'S WAGE PACKET

The Ultimate Irish Sports Fan knows there's only one solution to the chronic problems that beset Irish football: cut John Delaney's wages. His wages are standing in the way of Ireland playing like Spain, and a vibrant League of Ireland being able to compete at Champions League level.

ALLOW MR DELANEY TO BUY YOU A PINT IN EASTERN EUROPE

The disdain expressed above can be cured with a free drink in a karaoke bar in Tallinn/Moscow/Warsaw paid for out of said FAI chief executive's said hefty wage packet hours after a famous Irish draw.

KNOW THE TWO GREATEST PERFORMANCES IN THE HISTORY OF FOOTBALL

Never mind Messi, Ronaldo, Pelé or Maradona. If anyone asks you, the two greatest performances of all time were Paul McGrath for Ireland against Italy in 1994 and Roy Keane for ManU against Juventus in Turin in 1999. Even if you haven't seen either game – and you suspect that at least one has been over-hyped and is now just a shorthand media cliché – you must insist that these displays are unmatched by anything else in football. Talk about how a crocked McGrath didn't give Baggio a sniff all game. And about how Roy got booked and knew he was going to miss the final, yet still, with almost divine selflessness, 'pounded every blade of grass' (essential phrase).

GET INVOLVED IN A TWITTER SLAGGING MATCH WITH JOE BROLLY

Argue with Joe over a rule change or his analysis of a match or – if you're from Cavan – throw out a few choice comments about your own county. Don't start a crusade against his organ donation campaign – you'll look needlessly mean. If Brolly chooses not to engage, try Colm Parkinson or Ewan MacKenna instead.

KEEP AN EYE OUT FOR MLS PLAYERS WITH IRISH SURNAMES

This is a modern one. Robbie's former teammate Mike Magee and Maurice Fitz's nephew Shane O'Neill are two players we need to be alive to. Jack Charlton used to sniff around Oxford United's poky ground to find the grandsons of adventurous Irish grannies. It turns out his harnessing of the granny rule only scraped the surface. O'Neill and Keane should be heading for LA.

ARGUE THAT IRELAND WOULD HAVE WON EURO '92 IF WE HAD QUALIFIED

The fact that Denmark eventually won the tournament only confirmed to the red-blooded Irish sports fan that we would have won the thing had we not frittered away qualification to an entirely useless England team. If only a civil war had broken out in England rather than Yugoslavia, Ireland would have got in there. Yes, Euro '92 is frequently regarded as the one that got away. Despite the fact that we qualified for every tournament around it, and despite the fact that in Euro '88 we were eight minutes away from reaching the semis and knocking the eventual winners out, this is still the one that we could have won.

TELL LOTS OF ANECDOTES ABOUT MOSS KEANE

Whenever there's an after-dinner story told about Irish rugby, Mossie's name is never far away. Classic of the genre: 1970s Leinster out-half Mick Quinn and his Munster counterpart Tony Ward are drinking in the Lansdowne club bar (the perfect scene for a Mossie anecdote). Mossie is there too. Mossie shouts in Wardy's ear that he is the 'best out-half I have ever played with'. Quinn overhears this and corners Mossie near the toilets. 'So yer man up there is the best out-half you ever played with?' Moss replies, 'Not at all, Quinny. You are, by far. It's just that I have to play with the little b****cks for Munster.'

GROUSE ABOUT THE CATEGORISATION OF NORTHERN IRISH ATHLETES BY THE BRITISH MEDIA

Whenever the issue of a Norn Iron sportsman's tribal identity is brought up, allude to the classic BBC commentators' practice of referring to him as 'British' when he wins a world championship/major and a 'plucky little Irishman' when he loses/misses the cut. It's a long-standing complaint, but one that survives. Eddie Irvine and Barry McGuigan were dragooned into the UK's embrace after stirring victories and shunned as gallant Irish fellows after bad losses.

INSIST THAT OUR 1982 WORLD CUP CONTENDERS WERE BETTER THAN ANY OF JACK'S TEAMS

Robbed in Paris and Brussels. The Irish team that almost qualified in 1982 were in an absurdly hard group with France, Belgium and Holland. They managed to push Holland – finalists in the two previous World Cups – into fourth place in the group, defeating the Dutch and the French in Dublin. However, they lost out to Belgium in Brussels thanks to a referee who may or may not have been bribed, and then Kevin Moran was penalised for a phantom hand-ball in Paris.

DISMISS THE QUALITY OF THE AVIVA PREMIERSHIP AT ANY OPPORTUNITY

Whenever you refer to the Aviva Premiership, remark on how boring and inferior it is. Preface it with adjectives: the 'turgid Aviva Premiership' or the 'mind-numbing Aviva Premiership'. Always say 'Aviva' – mentioning the sponsor diminishes its grandeur.
Get more aggressive in your dismissals on internet forums where English posters are questioning the competitiveness of the Pro12.

ANTICIPATE THE ENGLISH MEDIA'S OVERHYPING OF THEIR COUNTRY'S CHANCES AHEAD OF A MAJOR TOURNAMENT

Set your eyes to permanent eye-roll for this one. You are not anti-English – it's just that their blaring and inexplicably cocky tabloid media turns you off big time. (Try to forget about the Irish media's cheerleading in the lead-up to Euro 2012.)

NEVER UTTER A FOUL WORD ABOUT PAUL MCGRATH, KEVIN MORAN OR JOHN HAYES

Anyone else can be taken down a peg or two with relative impunity. These three men, however – more than anyone else in Irish sport – emit a saintly aura. They are people's men to the core, humble and self-effacing.

Tea and the GAA
A Love Affair

You can forget about your pints of the black stuff and park your alcopops. There is one official beverage of the GAA, and its name is tea. In flasks, in lucky mugs, in paper cups: tea is sacramentally imbibed by Gaels before, in the middle of, and at the end of every GAA match.

Sometimes you'd wonder if Gaelic games exist purely as a socially appropriate way for men to drink tea outdoors in the company of other men. Forget about paying inter-county players – the greatest existential threat to the GAA is a global tea blight. Coffee could never fill its void.

Nothing says summer in Ireland like two lads having their tea and ham sandwiches up against a wall before a match. The man on the right needs two plastic bags for all his lunch supplies.

In America, there's a tradition called 'tailgating', whereby sports fans hang out in the stadium car park before games, drinking beers from the trunks of their cars and acting rowdy. That wouldn't interest these fellas. They're just happy to drink tea from their favourite mugs and talk livestock.

we've established, tea is a serious siness. This prankster, though, es to rock the boat. Upside-down ps. What are you like.

There's work to do somewhere, no doubt, but it can wait. Because there's tea to drink and buns to eat.

A love of tea is passed down from generation to generation, as this photo from Parnell Park proves. Blood is thicker than water, but is it thicker than tea? Probably depends how much milk you're taking ...

Such is the insatiable demand for tea at Connaught football matches that stewards are forced to wear numbered tea bibs in order to prevent the massive tea urns from being looted of their precious juice.

The most powerful person at any GAA ground is not the club chairman or the manager or the provincial chief: it's the tea lady. She calls the shots. Some tea women are more authoritarian than others. This lady insists that the umpires and linesmen sit in alternating order before a drop is poured.

Jack Charlton never comes to Ireland without his commemorative USA '94 mug. He's just not a paper cup kind of guy. (OK, it's not technically a GAA photo, but this demands inclusion.)

For the very rare occasion when tea is not enough, God invented whiskey.

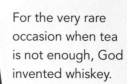

Hurling is the only sport in the world where thirty lads go hell for leather for seventy minutes, bashing each other with their sticks, and then sit down afterwards with a nice hot cup of tea.

The Greatest Ever
League of Ireland /
Pop Culture Crossovers

Look, the LOI isn't the sexiest organisation in the wide world of sports, but that's not to say its teams haven't penetrated the realms of popular culture. Far from it. LOI clubs have popped up in some remarkable places over the years. Here are our favourites.

WENDELL PIERCE & ST PAT'S

No LOI fan is as famous (or as random) as Wendell Pierce, who played cigar-chomping detective Bunk Moreland in *The Wire*. Pierce's affection for St Pat's is a by-product of Twitter: he was tweeting his love for his hometown NFL team, the New Orleans Saints, a few years back when some St Pat's supporters asked him if he also supported the SuperSaints. The bond remains unbroken to this day. Watching Pierce's Twitter feed light up with pro-St Pat's tweets during the 2014 FAI Cup final day was a joyful experience.

JOHNNY LOGAN & BOHEMIANS

Never have Ireland's two great passions – sport and the Eurovision – been fused in a marriage as beautiful of that of Bohs and Johnny Logan. Bohs supporters adopted 'Hold Me Now' ahead of a UEFA Cup thrashing in Norway in the early noughties, and Logan decided to embrace the affection of Gypsies' supporters. He even sang at Kevin Hunt's testimonial at Dalymount. 'I've never quite experienced the love that you feel from the Bohs people,' Logan told *The Craig Doyle Show* back in 2012. Long may it last.

RATS & ROVERS

Paths to Freedom was the brilliant RTÉ turn-of-the-century mockumentary that followed Raymond 'Rats from the Flats' Doyle (Michael McElhatton), a rapper-poet trying to piece his life together after getting out of the 'Joy. The lovable rogue loved nothing more than to wear his signed Shamrock Rovers jersey while reciting poetry.

A sample of his work: *Adolf Hitler, Pinochet / I hope you have a lovely day / Pol Pot, Maggie Thatcher / Now I'm going to get me scratcher.*

MAUREEN O'HARA & ROVERS

Maureen O'Hara is one of Ireland's most famous exports. Born in Ranelagh and beloved in Tinseltown, O'Hara's links to the LOI are perhaps less celebrated. Her father was an early investor in Shamrock Rovers, and O'Hara is a lifelong supporter of the club. In 1957 she was featured on *This Is Your Life*; her favourite Rovers player from her youth, centre-half Joe Williams, was flown to Hollywood and introduced by the presenter as 'one of the greatest players in the history of international soccer football'. Fair play to him.

THE BEAUTIFUL SOUTH & CORK CITY

You can make the case that the 1989 Cork City jersey is the greatest kit in the history of the League of Ireland: it's a riff on the trailblazing Germany Euro '88 jersey that's only improved by Cork's superior colour scheme. And who isn't nostalgic for the old stencilled Guinness logo? Still, the last place anyone expected the jersey to turn up was in the music video for The Beautiful South's 'Prettiest Eyes' in 1994. We're not totally sure how much of an honour this is ... Still, it's better than the Leesiders' other pop-culture claim to fame: the blink-and-you'll-miss-it shot of a guy in Goa wearing the shorts from the 2003 Cork City kit in *The Bourne Supremacy*.

THE LIFE & TIMES OF TIM & KILDARE COUNTY

In 2008, a brilliant new adult cartoon (sorry, animated series) debuted on HBO. It chronicled the misadventures of Tim, a twenty-something urbanite. There were lots of odd moments on the show, but none as surreal as when Tim and his buddies walked into a local tavern that had a Kildare County poster on its bathroom door. Why? Who cares. It's by far the coolest thing ever associated with the Newbridge club that was founded in 2002 and disbanded in 2009.

DUSTIN THE TURKEY & ST FRANCIS

Before he disgraced the nation at the Eurovision, Dustin the Turkey was a failed Irish presidential candidate. Interestingly, he chose to promote his 'man of the people' values by being photographed in his beloved St Francis jersey in his election literature. St Francis would leave the League after the 2000–01 season, and Dustin ... Well, we know what happened to him.

ST. FRANCIS F.C.
VENI VIDI VICI
Founded 1958

DREAM TEAM & SHELBOURNE

In the late 1990s Sky 1's first attempt at home-grown drama was the football-based drama *Dream Team*, which followed the trials and tribs of the fictional side Harchester United. After years of struggle, Harchester qualified for the UEFA Cup where they were drawn against Shelbourne. The teams played to a stalemate, but Shels lost on penalties, which presumably cost the fictional Ollie Byrne thousands.

NICKY BYRNE & COBH

Loathe as we are to celebrate any of Ireland's boy band members, it would be journalistically negligent if we failed to mention Nicky Byrne's pre-Westlife career with Cobh Ramblers and St Francis's. A goalie for Home Farm who went on to Leeds, Byrne returned to Ireland and eventually wound up in Cork as Cobh's keeper for eleven games in 1998. Our (and society's) major regret is that Byrne wasn't good enough in goal to eke out a footballing career. A year later, he met Louis Walsh, and the rest, sadly, is history.

THE UNDERTONES & DERRY CITY

Not only can Derry City count members of the Undertones amongst their fans, the club has even been featured on the cover of the band's 7-inch single 'My Perfect Cousin' from 1980. It might look like generic Subbuteo, but we know it's Derry. In return, the fans murder 'Teenage Kicks' every week.

CHARLO & BOHS/PAT'S

In 1994, Roddy Doyle wrote *Family*, a series for RTÉ/BBC that centred on the Spencers. In the first episode, arsehole dad Charlo brings his son, complete with Liverpool scarf, to see Bohs and Pat's play in Dalymount Park.

Unleashing
the Beast:
Rugby Spirit Animals

New Agers believe that the spirit of an animal lurks deep inside every human. Here, we have tuned in our own mystical antennas to identify the animals within some of Ireland's best rugby players.

PAULIE: THE GRIZZLY BEAR

At rest, Paul O'Connell has the cuddly gruffness of a cub. In the heat of battle, though, he is transformed into the grizzly bear. Fearsome and indomitable, he is unparalleled amongst second rows. His hunger for battle is unquenchable.

BOD:
THE BALD EAGLE

The king of all it surveys. A sight to behold in full flight, with wings spread. An imperious creature, possessing rare grandeur.

ROG: THE SALMON

The journey of the Atlantic salmon over its lifespan is mind-boggling: it makes a trek across the ocean before swimming up a river, against the current, to spawn. Ronan O'Gara brought all of the salmon's spirit of courage to the rugby pitch. He wasn't the biggest creature in his habitat, but his performances were often extraordinary.

STRINGER: THE MEERKAT

Diminutive but fierce and wily, Peter Stringer extracts his genius from his inner meerkat. Stringer has far more in common with these short-haired mammals found in the deserts of southern Africa than just stature. Scientists have noted that the meerkat can dig through its own weight in sand in seconds. With equal stealth, Stringer can shovel through a mass of limbs at the ruck to hoover up the ball and fire a bullet pass to his waiting outhalf.

THE KEARNEYS: ALSATIANS

If you encountered them in an unexpected place, like a dark alley, you might naturally fear them. But in truth, Rob and Dave, like Alsatians, are playful and inoffensive. In fact they're so tame, you could grow quite bored in their presence.

27

WOODIE: THE OWL

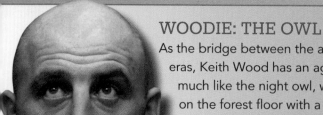

As the bridge between the amateur and professional eras, Keith Wood has an ageless majesty about him – much like the night owl, which surveys the goings-on on the forest floor with a hard-earned scepticism. Woodie has a ferocious streak too, dining on front rows like hapless mice.

HENDERSON: THE LLAMA

Maybe it's just his long face, but Iain Henderson seems to have the most easily recognisable spirit animal: at an Ireland camp in 2013, Donncha O'Callaghan, Ireland's spirit-animal whisperer, proclaimed to Hendo: 'You're a llama!' Llamas are known for their elegant wool and graceful posture, but zoologists have noted that some possess a streak called 'berserk llama syndrome', where they display dangerously aggressive behaviour towards other humans. Perhaps this explains Henderson's ferocity on the pitch.

SEANIE: THE HIPPOPOTAMUS

Given Sean O'Brien's passion for agriculture, some might think there's a bull inside Carlow's beast of the rugby pitch. But in truth, his animal spirit emerges from somewhere deeper in the jungle. Large and deceptively fast, O'Brien – especially with the ball in hand in open field – is all hippo. Like a good hippopotamus, he also has an affinity for water, as displayed during the 2013 Lions tour.

SEXTON: THE SHARK

Dig deep into Johnny Sexton's personality, as many journalists have done, and you won't find a joyful raconteur or a messer. No, Sexton is a shark, driven by a steely determination towards victory.

HICKIE: THE LEOPARD

With the ball in hand and the field opening out before him, Denis Hickie could not be caught. Like the leopard, he was always the fastest beast on the pitch. Flash back to France v Ireland 1999, and Dal Maso surging towards the try line. Out of nowhere comes Hickie, devouring the distance. The poor Frenchman was an antelope caught in Hickie's tracks.

HAYES: THE BULL

Another Irish rugby legend who wears his spirit animal on his sleeve. John Hayes always preferred the pastures of west Limerick to the rugby pitch. The Bull played tight head with a rugged virility.

BIG DEV: THE BRONTOSAURUS

A giraffe might be the obvious choice for Devin Toner, but in fact he possesses an animal spirit far more gigantic. The brontosaurus is both huge and uncannily gentle. Just as it loved nothing more than munching on treetops, so too does Toner fully enter his element when he is hoisted above the lineout, fifty feet in the sky.

Nearly

100 Things

That Only GAA People Say

A select few sayings and phrases have become enshrined in the vernacular of the GAA's media, players and public. We don't know how they got there, but we know they're not going away. Here are nearly a hundred of our favourite GAA clichés. Some of them are stock sayings by Cyril Farrell and Ger Canning. Some are things you hear from auld lads in the terrace at a club match. Some you hear from the county manager or captain after a match. Combined, they make up the odd and illuminating vocabulary of the GAA.

STUFF ONLY GAA FANS SAY

'CHAMPIONS LEAGUE–STYLE FORMAT'

Let's face it, if Michael Cusack and the lads were inventing the GAA today and someone proposed the current provisional championship format – with some teams playing for four consecutive weeks and others going nearly two months without a game – the majority would say, 'No, that sounds shit.' Every Gael dreams of the introduction of the Champions League–style format. Not that they'll every see it brought in.

'THEY'VE ANOTHER FIFTEEN ON THE LINE THAT ARE AS GOOD'
Regularly said about Kilkenny's hurlers, and now Dublin's footballers. Often followed by the words '... if not better'.

'THE TOWN END'
Every non-urban GAA ground has one.

'THE GAA LOVE A DRAW'

'PUT IT UP'
Usually shouted from the crowd towards an umpire when an insurance point goes over the bar.

'HE OWES HIS COUNTY NOTHING'
It is criminal to talk about John Mullane without using this cliché.

'HE WAS A GREAT MINOR, BUT THEN THE DRINK GOT HIM'
The most common (and probably correct) explanation for why blazing underage talent burns out before turning twenty-five.

'WHERE'S YOUR PENCIL, REF?'

'BEND YOUR BACK'
Usually said to a new underage player who has played a lot of soccer but not much GAA and has a tendency to dribble the ball 'soccer style'.

'SURE HE'S SHITE'
Heard at a club game when there's a much-heralded county player on the pitch.

'LIKE HITTING A BALL OFF A STONE WALL'
Don't aim the ball at Tommy Walsh. It's just going to come straight back at you.

'ONE OF YIS'

'HE'S GOOD, BUT THE BROTHER IS BETTER'
How often did we hear this about Alan and Bernard Brogan? Or Seamus and Aidan O'Shea?

'THE GRAB-ALL ASSOCIATION'
An alternative interpretation of the GAA acronym. Regularly exclaimed by someone who thinks he is the first person ever to say it.

'AH REF, THIS IS CHAMPIONSHIP'
Mostly heard in local games when the ref gives a soft free that would have been OK in the league. The set of rules used for Championship is totally different.

'CLOSE THE GATES'
Uttered at club games when one local rival is hammering another. Usually followed by '... and make them watch'.

'HOW'S HE ON THE COUNTY PANEL?

'ARE YA WATCHIN' THE MINORS?'

The only reason for going to the minor game rather than staying in the pub is that you have a relative playing. And even then, you turn up begrudgingly.

'CLOSE THE GATES'

'IT'LL BE GRAND, SURE WE'LL GET TICKETS OUTSIDE QUINNS'

The cocky refrain of a ticketless Mayo, Kerry or Donegal fan in the queue for Flannery's the night before the All-Ireland.

'SURE WE'VE GOT THE WIND IN THE SECOND HALF'

'IT'S ONLY THE LEAGUE'

In the end, it's all about the Championship. If your county loses by twelve points at home while playing an experimental line-up that features your second-string goalkeeper at full forward, take heart: it's only the league.

'YOU CAN'T BE BLOWING FOR EVERYTHING'

Can be preceded or followed by 'seriously, ref!'

'THEY'RE FLYING IN TRAINING'

When it comes to Championship football and hurling, there is often little evidence regarding the form of teams. So hearing that a team is doing well in training is highly prized information. It's unclear how 'flight' is measured, or by whom.

'COULD HAVE USED HAWKEYE THERE'

The sad refrain of many a supporter at a club match, when a kick that crosses the posts totally baffles a ref and his umpires.

STUFF ONLY GAA PLAYERS AND MANAGERS SAY

'LOOKIT'

A multi-purpose verbal crutch utilised by GAA players up and down the country when being interviewed in the media. It can be used to buy time as they search for an answer that won't get them thrown off the panel. Equally, it can be uttered menacingly at the beginning of a sentence to reinforce a point.

'A DRAW WAS THE RIGHT RESULT IN THE END'

Said after a highly competitive and entertaining game, usually because 'neither team deserved to lose'.

'WE WILL BE USING SUBS'

'WHAT DO YOU THINK OF THAT, JOE BROLLY?'

Perhaps the most modern GAA cliché.

'THEY WROTE US OFF DURING THE WEEK'

A common potshot by triumphant managers at members of the radio and press corps who offered fair-to-middling criticism of their team.

'WE WON'T BE TAKING THEM FOR GRANTED'

'SEPTEMBER'

The mythical month known by only four GAA teams a year. The thought of gracing Croker when the autumn sunlight shines warmly over the stands lifts every inter-county player through the January slog.

'DIRTY BALL'

Dirty ball is usually seen around the middle of the field and two inches off the ground. Won by the Richie McCaws of the team.

'SEMI-FINALS ARE FOR WINNING'

A great excuse for playing crap in a semi-final.

'SURE TOG OUT ANYWAY'

'SAVE A FEW OF THOSE FOR THE GAME'

At the end of the day, you've only got so many points in your locker, so you can't be wasting them on training.

STUFF ONLY GAA PUNDITS AND COMMENTATORS SAY

'THREE WISE MEN'

Most often seen stalking the sidelines at very successful inter-county sides. Some classic examples include Brian Cody, Michael Dempsey and Martin Fogarty at Kilkenny. And Ger Loughnane, Mike McNamara and Tony Considine at Clare. As a collective, they must be likened to the mystics who delivered gifts to the baby Jesus. It's unclear why GAA back-room teams don't quite work in four-somes, and there was always something unconvincing about the Mickey Moran/John Morrison tandem in the noughties.

'MAJESTIC MACGILLYCUDDY'S REEKS'

A game, especially if it's a Munster football final at the height of summer, cannot be broadcast from Killarney without mention of the 'Majestic MacGillycuddy's Reeks'. On Sundays in July, the sun is often found splitting the rocks of said mountain range.

It is a little-known fact that failure by broadcasters to mention the majestic nature of these mountains will likely result in a beating with a large stick by Weeshie Fogarty.

'EXPONENT'

A go-to adjective for broadcasters to describe players that dates back to Michael O'Hehir's days doing commentary. Usually preceded by the words 'one of the finest' and followed by 'the art of high fielding' or 'the art of the cross-field kick'. It is frowned upon to talk about Mick O'Connell without describing him as an exponent of many of the game's finer skills.

'THE SPIRITUAL LEADER'

Not always the best player on a team, and normally not the captain either, but clearly the most inspirational member of the panel. The one teammates look to at low moments; someone who will speak up and help 'drive them on'. This is not the person who leads the decade of the rosary – that would be the team priest. Donal Óg Cusack is your classic spiritual leader.

'DUMMY TEAM'

A menace to GAA match programme buyers countrywide. These days, you're behind tactically unless you're changing your line-up just minutes before the throw-in.

'THE GAME TOOK ON A LIFE OF ITS OWN'

'QUARTERBACK'

Soccer pundits first used this Yankcentric phrase to describe the role performed by Xabi Alonso or Michael Carrick, players who sit deep and spray around passes, and now it has also entered the GAA lexicon. Deployed often in reference to Stephen Cluxton, due to the importance of his kickouts in Dublin's game plan. We patiently await the day when NFL analysts start talking about someone playing the 'Mark McHugh role' in American football.

'TIGHT PITCH'

According to the rules of the game, all GAA pitches are of a standard size. But GAA fans know that's not the case. A tight pitch is the toughest place to go: there's no space to play, and the opposition fans are right on top of you. It's generally cited as a factor for the underdog having a chance. Two famously tight pitches are St Conleth's Park in Newbridge and Nowlan Park in Kilkenny.

'THE HARD YARDS'

'WIDE-OPEN SPACES'

The opposite of the tight pitch. The underdog fears the wide-open spaces of Croke Park and Semple Stadium that always seem to be opening up.

'HE TOOK THE SENSIBLE OPTION'

When it comes down to brass tacks, we Irish are pragmatic, and no more so than when faced with the option of a one-on-one with an opposing goalie from a difficult angle. Alan Dillon – the textbook definition of a sensible footballer – never blazes the ball at the top corner of the net. No, he takes 'the sensible option'.

'DRESSING ROOM WALL MATERIAL'

In the build-up to a game, any slight against the opposition is ripe to be pinned to the dressing room wall and used as fuel to push a team towards victory.

'THEY HAD THEIR CHANCE ON THE FIRST DAY'

An underdog has one opportunity to win, and that's in the first game. If it goes to a replay, they don't stand a chance. When it's said after Kilkenny win an All-Ireland hurling replay, you can turn off the telly.

'YOU DON'T WIN ALL-IRELANDS IN JULY'

'GONE TO THE WELL'

When it comes to crunch time in the Championship, you don't just dig deep, you go to the well. No team has gone to the well more down the years than Brian Cody and Kilkenny, particularly before said All-Ireland final replay.

'MEATH WON'T FEAR THE DUBS'

It's probably time they started to. They've beaten them once in a decade.

'UNDER THE RADAR'

Generally said around the All-Ireland

quarter-finals stage about a team that has quietly progressed through the qualifiers but hasn't had much press coverage.

'A WIDE IS AS GOOD AS A POINT AT THIS STAGE'

The most ridiculous, bullshit GAA cliché of all time. It remains prevalent even in the age of analytics and sports science.

'WAITING IN THE LONG GRASS'

A cousin to 'under the radar', heard in the build-up to a game when a team is being underrated and plotting an ambush. Most often uttered by Cyril Farrell.

'THE UMPIRE TOOK UP A GOOD POSITION'

'RATIFIED'

Heard on bulletins across the country in October and November following news that a manager has been appointed. 'That's the smile of a ratified man from Ger Cunningham.' GAA and international treaties: the only places where this word is used.

'DING-DONG BATTLE'

The O'Sheas and the Cavanaghs, a classic 'ding-dong battle'.

'FORTRESSES'

All away tests are formidable in inter-county GAA, but some grounds have taken on the status of medieval battle camps. Aughrim has proven to be a fortress for Wicklow. Perhaps because of the travel required to London, Ruislip has also taken on fortress-like status in recent years.

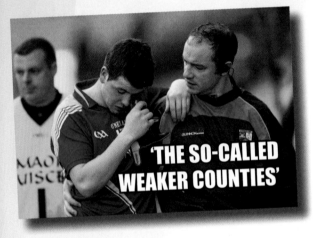

'THE SO-CALLED WEAKER COUNTIES'

'THE SHACKLES ARE OFF'

Why were they on in the first place? And who put them on?

'WRISTY HURLER'

The finest compliment to bestow upon a player. Bubbles O'Dwyer is the wristiest hurler going.

'SOCCER-STYLE'

You'll hear commentators say this anytime the ball isn't kicked from the hands or punched into the net. Also when someone decides to do some 'soccer-style' dribbling.

'THEY PLAYED LIKE MEN POSSESSED'

'AND THEN SHANE CURRAN TOOK IT UPON HIMSELF TO ...'

No match report from a game featuring Shane Curran – be it for Roscommon or St Brigid's – is complete without the words 'and then Shane Curran took it upon himself to ...' It will normally be followed by descriptions of Curran moonwalking out from goal/soloing for 100 metres/pulling an actual rabbit out from under his jersey before saving a penalty.

'YOU'VE GOT TO LOSE ONE TO WIN ONE'

'THE SO-CALLED WEAKER COUNTIES'

Leitrim, Wicklow, Carlow, Longford ...

'THE SYSTEM'

Jim McGuinness invented The System. Donegal played The System. Many have tried to implement The System. Pundits call it The System because they're not quite sure what it is. The System even has its own Wikipedia page.

'KILKENNY TRAINING GAMES'

A cliché as well as a myth. Kilkenny training games are harder than most Championship matches. Where else would you get Tommy Walsh and Henry Shefflin knocking lumps out of each other?

'HE SWALLOWED THE WHISTLE'

Regularly said about Brian Cody's refereeing style during Kilkenny training matches.

'THEY DIED WITH THEIR BOOTS ON'

A favourite of Gaels raised on WWII films. Refers to a team that loses but leaves it all on the pitch, like Limerick against Kilkenny in the 2014 All-Ireland semi-final.

THE GAA WINNERS SPEECH

Every decade, a Joe Connolly or a Seán Óg Ó hAilpín gives a glorious sermon, but by and large the victory speech is just the final annoying delay before the victory celebrations can begin. The typical speech is a litany of clichés, which we present to you now in chronological order.

'A HUACHTARÁN, UACHTARÁN CHUMANN LÚTHCHLEAS GAEL, TAOISEACH ...'

No great (or even mediocre) speech can begin without dropping a cúpla focal as an act of deference to the assembled dignitaries and GAA bureaucrats.

'TO THE SPONSORS: WE COULDN'T HAVE DONE IT WITHOUT YOU, LADS'

There is no greater faux pas than to omit mention of the team sponsor. And while you're at it, thank the bus company, the restaurant that provides the post-match carvery, the water-bottle supplier, and the lady who makes the tea.

'TO THE TEAM THEMSELVES: LADS, NO ONE WOULD HAVE THOUGHT WE COULD DO THIS IN DECEMBER'

And don't forget the subs who drove the starters on in training.

AND TO THE MANAGER: WELL, WHAT IS THERE TO SAY ABOUT HIM THAT HASN'T ALREADY BEEN SAID?'

Praise the lad without giving away how much you've been slagging him behind his back.

'FINALLY, THREE CHEERS FOR THE LOSERS. HIP HIP!'

The celebrations cannot really begin until the captain has issued some sort of semi-patronising acknowledgement to the losing side.

CONCLUSION: 'SEE YOU IN COPPERS!' (OR SUBSTITUTE NAME OF LOCAL DISCO)

THE FOUR STAGES OF A GAA FIGHT

DEFCON 4: 'HANDBAGS' Just two lads letting off steam.

DEFCON 3: 'SCHEMOZZLE' A potentially violent altercation eventually brought under control that has a comedic and even charming quality.

DEFCON 2: 'MELEE' See All-Ireland final 1996.

DEFCON 1: 'SHAMEFUL SCENES' A fight that spills over to include members of the public, stray animals, umpires. Fodder for *Liveline* discussions.

The Gary Mackay
Hall of Fame

The Gary Mackay Hall of Fame is a non-profit organisation honouring the non-Irish players who inadvertently helped Ireland down through the years. To be clear: it does not honour those who have played poorly against Ireland; rather those who have performed great deeds in games not involving Ireland that accidentally helped the Irish cause.

GARY MACKAY (1987)

It was Mackay, a Scot, who ushered in a glorious era for Irish football when he scored a late winner against Bulgaria in a European Championship qualifier at the end of 1987, thus guaranteeing Ireland's qualification for Euro '88. Ray Houghton's headed goal in Stuttgart (and Christy Moore's raucous song about it) would not have been possible without Mackay's goal. Indeed, it's likely that the subsequent seven years of Irish football – Eamon Dunphy slinging his pen, Packie Bonner saving from Daniel Timofte, Mick Byrne meeting the Pope, the Three Amigos, even Harry's Challenge – would not have happened had this unheralded Scottish centre-forward not got the ball rolling by scuffing his shot home in Sofia.

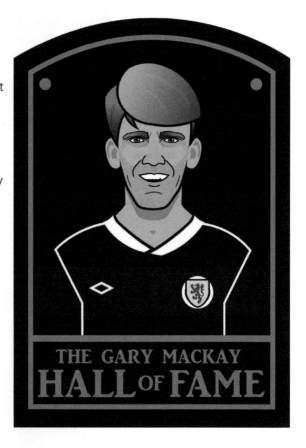

THE GARY MACKAY
HALL OF FAME

MONIQUE (1990)

Let us stop to honour the forgotten heroine of Italia '90; she who FIFA boss Sepp Blatter tasked with carrying out the final part of Italia 90's Round of 16. The odds were against us. The Netherlands and Ireland were in one pot, West Germany and Romania were in the other. Many dreaded that we would be drawn against the eventual tournament champions, but Monique delivered: she drew Holland and Germany together, leaving us with Romania.

Who was Monique? An up-and-coming FIFA bureaucrat from Zurich? An aspiring Italo pop starlet? Blatter's niece? Sepp told the gathered media that she was 'one of the ladies here who are not involved in any way in the competition'. Thank you again, Monique, whoever you are.

SANTIAGO CAÑIZARES (1993)

On the night of November 17, 1993, the fate of Group 3 was balanced on a knife edge. Spain hosted the reigning European champions, Denmark, while Ireland were otherwise engaged at Windsor Park. All three were chasing World Cup qualification. Early on in Seville, Spain's veteran goalkeeper, Andoni Zubizarreta, was sent off and Cañizares, who'd never been capped, thrown into goal. As football writer Rob Smyth wrote, 'As he walked onto the pitch, Cañizares went into a zone that he arguably did not enter for the rest of his career.'

Cañizares made save after amazing save, and with each, a feeling of foreboding descended upon the Danes. Alan McLoughlin would equalise in Belfast, Spain would win, and Ireland would be on their way to the USA. Gracias, Santiago.

ZBIGNIEW BONIEK (2011)

Polish legend Zbigniew Boniek must have remembered the longstanding affinity between Ireland and Poland when he got the call from UEFA to draw names out of the pot for the Euro 2012 qualification playoffs. With tricky trips to Turkey and Bosnia in play, Boniek inspired a very loud cry of 'YES!' from the nation when he pulled Estonia from the UEFA's goldfish bowl.

Ireland's 4-0 hammering of Estonia in Tallinn was not just the best result of the Trap years, it was also a dress rehearsal for the shenaniganism that would infect the Irish male in Poland the following summer. (Remember the Cork lads who snuck into the stadium and pretended to be ballboys?) For that, Zibi, we salute you.

LEONARDO SARTO (2014, 2015)

An Italian rugby player served the cause of Ireland not once but twice during the Joe Schmidt era. Our Six Nations championships in 2013 and 2014 might not have happened without the Kipling-esque heroism of Signore Sarto.

On the last day of the 2014 Six Nations, England needed a 51-point win in the Stadio Olimpico to bring the Championship home. Les Rosbifs were up 39 points with 12 minutes remaining and paradise was in sight … That is, until Sarto intercepted a lazy Joe Launchbury pass and scored the try that halted the momentum of the beefy, irresistible English war machine.

Twelve months later, the Welsh were in Rome on the ultimate day of the Six Nations, attempting to hockey the Italians and set an extremely intimidating target for those who came later on. For the second year in a row, Sarto went on a one-man mission and dived into the corner to score a remarkable try at the death to keep the Welsh in check. What a hero.

RORY KOCKOTT (2015)

The latest entrant to the GMHOF is a man born in a place called East London in South Africa. On 21 March 2015, a magically unhinged France put forth many heroes in attack and many villains in defence. However, at the end of the day, only one man exploded with joy at the realisation that France had (just about) kept England's margin of victory below 26 points.

After watching teammate Yoann Huget malevolently keep the game alive even though eighty minutes had elapsed, Kockott had enough empathy with his Irish brethren to accept a 20-point defeat and boot the ball out of play. A selfless and deeply appreciated act. Welcome to the Gary Mackay Hall of Fame, Rory.

Recreation
Transformation

Some Irish sportspeople seem to arrive fully formed. Consider lads like Brian Cody and Ronan O'Gara: their personalities feel like they were forged from some primal stew, and their outward appearances have always been more or less the same, bar some deepening facial lines and the odd receding hairline. But then there are the Irish sports stars who have undergone subtle (and not-so-subtle) transformations over the years; whose careers are not only a chronology of wins and losses but also a physical journey. Here we present them as they once were.

BOD

We know Brian O'Driscoll better than any other Irish sportsperson, but he is also one of the great chameleons of our time.

KEITH WOOD

Woodie is one of sport's most iconic bald men, but it's worth remembering that he wasn't always Uncle Fester. His locks were positively flowing in this photo from the 1994 Five Nations (left). And as far the photo below, well, it's hard to recognise him at all because he's covered head-to-toe in mud.

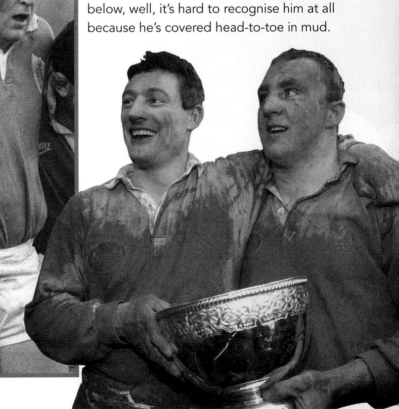

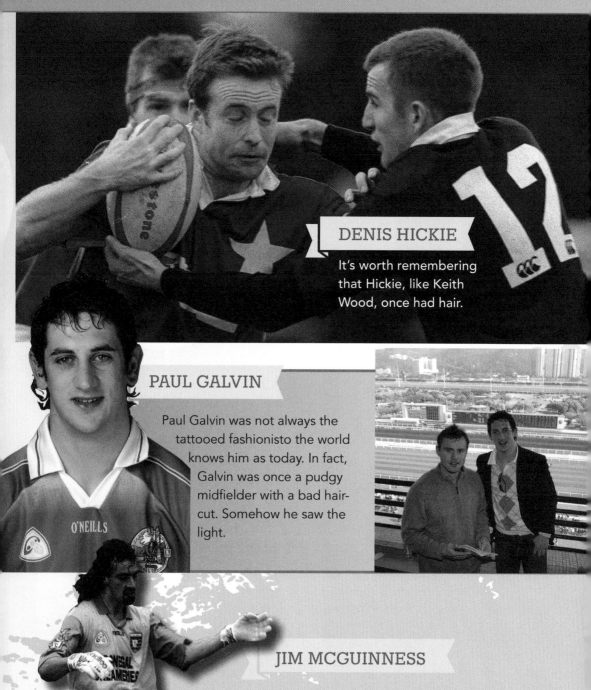

DENIS HICKIE

It's worth remembering that Hickie, like Keith Wood, once had hair.

PAUL GALVIN

Paul Galvin was not always the tattooed fashionisto the world knows him as today. In fact, Galvin was once a pudgy midfielder with a bad haircut. Somehow he saw the light.

JIM MCGUINNESS

Before McGuinness was the messiah of Donegal GAA, he was just a Gaelic footballer who looked like Jesus. Here's Jimmy during the 1999 Championship, breaking all kinds of GAA fashion laws.

GORDON D'ARCY

As we well know, Gordon D'Arcy has two looks: bearded and unbearded. But he's not quite himself with this crew cut at a 1999 'A' international against France.

ROY KEANE

Here we have Roy Keane not quite looking like himself – which is to say, here is Roy Keane smiling.

Find Yourself: 15
Irish Sports Fan
Stereotypes

THE NOSTALGIC LAD

Worships at the altars of Kerry 1975–86, Muhammad Ali and George Best. Finds it hard to believe that Messi could be better than Pelé. Mike Gibson and Dick Milliken keep Brian O'Driscoll out of his all-time Irish XV. Thinks that Con Houlihan is the greatest writer of all time and has repeated his quote about Paddy Cullen running back to his goal-line in 1978 'like a woman who smells a cake burning in the oven' approximately 1,450 times.

Reads: Always asks for *The Irish Press* in the newsagents, only to be reminded that it shut down in 1995. Ends up getting the *Indo*, though as far as he's concerned it's shite.

Says: 'Mick O'Connell/Jack O'Shea/Seán Purcell/Mikey Sheehy was a mighty player. That Aidan O'Shea/Michael Darragh Macauley/Colm Cooper/Bernard Brogan lad isn't a patch on him.'

THE CORPORATE HAWK

Miraculously manages to end up at all the big matches. Divides his time between Celtic Park, Old Trafford, Croke Park's Príomh section, the Aviva's hospitality suites and the K Club. Has played golf with at least three people intimately involved in the collapse of the Irish economy. The boot of his S-Class Merc is stuffed with golf umbrellas sponsored by various financial institutions. Has an Anglo Irish golf ball in his underwear drawer. Loves Ryder Cup Weekend more than anything else in the world.

Reads: *Indo* during the week; all the Sunday papers.
Says: 'Look, no one forced anyone to buy a house.'

THE CYNIC

Blames everything on 'officialdom'. Rolls his eyes whenever (and we mean *whenever*) there is a draw in a GAA match. Obsessed with money and the salaries of people within sport, namely John Delaney, Paraic Duffy, Giovanni Trapattoni, all footballers in the Premiership, and all GAA inter-county managers. Suspicious of high-profile GAA players who go around to clubs handing out medals, believing there 'must be a few pound in it for them'. Did not take a side during the Saipan business, preferring to blame the whole thing on the FAI in general.

Reads: Nothing.
Says: 'It'll be a draw now, wait 'til you see.'

THE SKY SPORTS LAD

Watches Sky Sports News the same way Wall Street types watch Bloomberg. Thinks football began in August 1992. Has developed an increasing respect for Gary Neville over the past couple of years and will comment under YouTube videos: 'I have to say, Gary Neville is talking a lot of sense here, and that's coming from a Liverpool fan.' Doesn't watch the GAA until the Dubs get to at least the All-Ireland semi-final. Has never heard of the hurling or football leagues. Knows of the League of Ireland but has no time for it.

Reads: *The Star.*
Says: 'We've the Scousers coming up this weekend … Imagine.'

THE LEAGUE OF IRELAND FAN

Advances the claims of LOI men wherever and whenever possible. A romantic, almost heroic individual, sensitive to the slights of those who are not League of Ireland people. Finds himself drawn into battles on online forums with individuals he knows as 'barstoolers'. Speaks about the old Shamrock Rovers ground in Milltown as if it were a cross between the San Siro and the Maracanã.

Reads: Extratime.ie.

Says: 'They should never have gotten rid of Brian Kerr.'

THE WOMAN WHO ONLY WATCHES RUGBY

Follows the Irish rugby team and the Irish clubs in the Heineken Cup passionately; has been doing so since the year 2000. Her favourite player is Tommy Bowe. Dislikes soccer players, often remarking that they go down too easily. Doesn't object to the GAA in quite the same way, but her interest is only sparked if her county is doing well or if one of her work colleagues/college friends is on the team.

Reads: Twitter and Facebook.

Says: 'Who's Simon Geoghegan?'

THE FOOTBALL HIPSTER

Hates nothing more than middling, mediocre Premiership teams. Frequently alludes to harmless English clubs like West Brom, Stoke and Middlesbrough in pejorative terms, using their very names as bywords for all that is ignorant and uncultured in modern life. By contrast, he speaks about a club like Rayo Vallecano with something approaching reverence. Pronounces the team name Espanyol as 'Eth-panyol'. For more detail, see page 93.

Reads: *The Blizzard*, Jonathan Wilson and intellectual tomes on Spanish sport.

Says: 'No, you were watching West Brom and Swansea, I suppose?'

THE MAN WHO STICKS HIS HEAD IN THE BACK OF INTERVIEWS

Stands militantly beside the Man of the Match, either roaring in approval at everything his hero says or staring blankly into the camera as if he has never seen one before. Entirely a creature of the GAA, and one whose day may have come and gone thanks to GAA safety regulations. Blindingly partisan and generally a bit of a 'yahoo' merchant, his analysis does not rise above *Up for the Match* levels. The type of insane local clubman of whom referees live in mortal fear; the bane of the RTÉ sideline reporter's existence.

Reads: The match programme, but only the middle where the line-up is printed. And if the ref is making a bollocks of it, he will look for his name so he can abuse him personally. After twenty minutes the programme is rolled up and stuffed in his back pocket, never to be read again.

Says: 'Aaahhh Boy Seánie McMahon Boyyyy!!!'

THE PESSIMISTIC MAMMY

Possesses the fatalistic streak imprinted on the DNA of all women born west of the Shannon between 1800 and 1965. Never believes Ireland will win; always is sure that Spain or the All Blacks will hammer us and that Liechtenstein or Namibia are waiting in the long grass to surprise us. As the opposing team strolls across the halfway line with the ball, even with the Irish defenders all in position, she will hiss and groan as if a goal is imminent. Intriguingly, the males in her family often believe her negativity impacts upon their team's performance. She has even been blamed on occasion for Ireland conceding goals.

Reads: Nothing sports-related. And she never will.

Says: 'They'll lose it now, wait 'til you see.'

THE WANNABE YANK

Did a J1 in Boston/Yonkers/San Fran and came back with a new-found passion for baseball/basketball/American football. Only watches sports on dodgy internet streams. Pronounces it 'deee-fence' and frequently uses the adjective 'clutch'. A fiend for statistics. Oddly good with computers.

Reads: *Sports Illustrated*, Grantland, anything by Bill Simmons.

Says: 'LeBron is great, but Kobe is more clutch.'

THE LEFT-WINGER

Supports any Spanish club that comes from a region with secessionist ambitions; the more obscure, the better. Has a special love for Athletic Bilbao and St Pauli. Used to like Barcelona until the Qataris started sponsoring their kit. Makes a point of supporting Boca Juniors against River Plate. Admires hurling without ever immersing himself in the game; is baffled by the recent rise of rugby. Despises Real Madrid.
Reads: Anything by Eduardo Galeano, Jimmy Burns or David Goldblatt.
Says: 'I see Franco's men are trying to buy La Liga again.'

THE GAMBLER

Collects insider tittle-tattle wherever he can get it. Crestfallen if a team gets a late goal, he feels a flash of anger when the commentator expresses his satisfaction that the losing team salvaged something from the game. Always quick to give minority sports their due, he has become a big fan of Twenty20 cricket in recent times.
Reads: *The Racing Post*, PaddyPower.com, the *Star*.
Says: 'It's a Wicklow junior quarter-final. They're priced at evens, but I know for a fact that half the lads they're playing were struck down with food poisoning the other day. You know what to do.'

THE ALLICADOO

Seen at Ireland rugby matches since God was a wee slip of a lad, in a sheepskin coat with a hip flask in the inside pocket. He and his white-collar ilk formed a high proportion of the crowd at Lansdowne back when Ireland were shit in the 90s, but now they are outnumbered by the Krystle girls and culchies who hopped aboard the rugby train in the Brian O'Driscoll era. He's more contented these days at club rugby matches, where he struts around in the club blazer and knows all the patrons. August 1995 remains the blackest month of his life: when rugby turned professional.
Reads: *The Irish Times*, *The Irish Times* and *The Irish Times*.
Says: 'What's Mick Moylett up to these days?'

THE UFC FAN

Spends his time debating with old-style pugilists who make casually disparaging remarks about the new sport. An ardent defender of Conor McGregor; shouted 'Who are ya?' at José Aldo at the McGregor-Aldo press event in Dublin. Throws out stats about UFC fighters who aren't called Conor McGregor with a speed and authority that intimidates the uninitiated.

Reads: Sherdog, *Bloody Elbow*.

Says: 'Don't get me wrong, but McGregor needs to work on his ground and pound if he's going to beat Aldo.'

THE HURLING PERSON

Never fails to remind people that hurling is the greatest game in the world. Thanks God every day for allowing him to be one of those chosen Gaels born in a hurling county. Deplores 'bogball'. Competes with fellow Hurling People to utter the most extreme superlative after a good match. Uses adjectives like 'wristy' and 'manly' a lot.

Reads: Donal Óg Cusack's columns, Enda McEvoy in the *Examiner*, Vincent Hogan in the *Irish Independent*.

Says: 'We need a different rule book for hurling than there is in football.'

Bitches on Pitches

Irish people love sports. Irish people love animals. And given the long tradition of dogs, cats, foxes, badgers, squirrels, pigeons and seagulls loitering on GAA pitches and rugby fields up and down the country, we can draw only one conclusion: animals love sports too.

For ten months of the year, Irish goats have it pretty good. But come the Championship, they take cover on the highest, craggiest ground possible, because they know that somewhere, there are local GAA supporters lurking with a can of spray paint. Here's a goat in Fermanagh colours getting taunted by Armagh fans in Clones ahead of the 2008 Ulster final.

Since retirement, Tony McEntee has established himself as a cold-eyed coach and analyst; during his playing career he brought the same unsentimental approach to dealing with invading animals. Here, at a club match for Crossmaglen around the turn of this century, he escorted a dog from the pitch by the scruff of its neck. The message is clear: animals have no place at Parnell Park.

DUBDOGS

In our exhaustive research for this book, we found that no dog wears the county colours with more pride than the Dublin dog. The sight of Poms in blue has been common on the Hill since Heffo took the reins back in the 70s.

So common is the sight of a stray dog on a GAA pitch that the appendix of the referees' handbook includes information on the proper way to apprehend a miscreant mutt and discard canine faeces. Textbook work here from Brian Gavin.

Fairyhouse: where even the dogs on the street take bets.

And it's not just Irish dogs
who have an interest in sport.

True GAA legends always
seem to know how to respond
in the presence of stray animals. Here's Owen Mulligan,
Dick Clerkin, John Mullane
and Seán Óg Ó hAilpín all
calmly discarding animals
from the playing field.

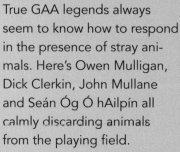

You think Mayo fans have it bad? How about their donkeys, who are forced to drag their despondent owners back west every September.

We're used to dogs, cats and pigeons, but there was something extraordinary about the sight of this fox on the RDS pitch at a Leinster-Ulster game in 2013.

When Specsavers announced their sponsorship of Hawkeye, the GAA celebrated by bringing a hawk to the pitch at Croker. Has a man ever been more comfortable in the company of a bird of prey than former GAA president Liam O'Neill?

Perhaps the most memorable canine invasion came during the 2004 Munster Senior Football final, when a dog ran onto the field as Stephen Lavin scored Limerick's only goal of the game. It's hard to know whether the crowd are cheering the goal or the dog for eluding ref Gerry Kinneavy.

We're pretty sure you wouldn't see a dingo running riot during a Collingwood match at the MCG, so you can imagine the consternation of our Australian cousins when this Jack Russell stormed the pitch during the second International Rules test at Croker back in 2004. Aussie Jude Bolton has no idea whether he should be playing the dog or the ball.

Technically this is not an Irish dog, but the experiences of this French collie are worth sharing. Back in 2002, Leinster paid a visit to Toulouse for a Heineken Cup match, and Lassie here decided get a better look at the Irish tyros. What did the Leinster players do? They found a spare jersey and draped it around the collie. And thus a lifelong Leinster fan was born.

Irish animals are not blinkered by gender when it comes to sprinting onto a pitch.

Have you ever seen a creature look more despondent at being hauled off a field of play? This guy really wanted a front-row seat.

Socks You Up:

A Tribute to GAA Players
Who Wear 'Em High

No part of the GAA wardrobe is as controversial or as psychologically revealing as the pair of socks pulled high. Numerous post-doc theses have been written about this phenomenon, but rarely has it been discussed in the media. It is a statement of style that only the game's true mavericks are willing to embrace. They are the brooding artists of the GAA: detached, enigmatic, lightning rods for criticism from the traditionalists.

CIARÁN MCDONALD, MAYO FOOTBALLER

The prototypical high-socked GAA player, McDonald has assumed near saintly status in retirement. In his playing days, he possessed all the attributes a player who insists on wearing his socks up needs to have if people are going to let him away with it. The cornrows and tattoos he sported in his later career were there merely to complement those high socks. Truly, an icon.

LATE-ERA PÁDRAIC JOYCE, GALWAY FOOTBALLER

Back when Galway were winning All-Irelands and Joyce was accompanied in their forward line by Michael Donnellan and Ja Fallon, he was a marksman of a full-forward. As such, he tended to wear his socks down. Late in his career, however, as Galway declined and he became more integral to their attack, he dropped into the centre-half forward playmaker role. He also changed the way he wore his socks. An ingenious move.

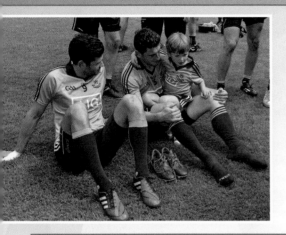

MODERN DUBLIN FOOTBALLERS

The bruisers who won the All-Ireland for Dublin in 1983 may not like it, but the county's modern forwards – in a nod to their status as the sexiest team in the game – are wearing their socks up in greater numbers. Bernard Brogan, Cian O'Sullivan and Paul Mannion are notable adherents. Cormac Costello satisfies himself with a kind of half-up job. Diarmuid Connolly isn't having it, however.

LAR CORBETT, TIPPERARY HURLER

As a neophyte corner forward in Tipp's All-Ireland winning 2001 side, Lar wasn't bold enough to chance the socks-up policy. However, as he became more prominent in the Liam Sheedy era, he pulled his socks up as a marker of his new stature. He who wears the high socks wears them bravely, and Lar has many of the classic foibles of socks-up players – such as dabbling with overly clever tactical gambits or writing a confessional autobiography – all of which prompt accusations of self-indulgence on and off the pitch.

CORK HURLING GOALKEEPERS

Cork hurling people are big on tradition, and modern Rebel County goalkeepers understand from the outset that their role entails rocking the socks-up look.

During his twenty-something-year reign as Cork's keeper, Ger Cunningham was one of the earliest proponents of the high sock. This tradition was continued by his successor, Donal Óg Cusack. Anthony Nash, who waited in the wings for Donal Óg to shuffle off, has stayed true to the tradition.

DJ CAREY, KILKENNY HURLER

DJ had that touch of tortured genius about him that often precipitates a socks-up policy, but he also had the elegance and class on the pitch to pull it off. Like fellow socks-up wearer Lar Corbett, he announced his retirement early but reneged on this decision before long. While there are always mitigating circumstances and other pressures involved in such a decision, it is nonetheless classic socks-up behaviour.

CERTAIN KERRY FOOTBALLERS

Even as the Kingdom's football under Éamonn Fitzmaurice has become more defensive, high-sock wearers can be found in abundance in the Kerry dressing room.

Colm Cooper is a classic case of adopting the socks-up style when one is moved into the centre-forward position. Kieran Donaghy is unusual; he opts for the socks-up look while operating in a traditional target man role.

David Moran is another fascinating case. He is a centre forward born in the body of a midfielder, as the 40-yard footpass he landed in the breadbasket of Kieran Donaghy in the 2014 All-Ireland semi-final against Mayo showed. His socks are always up.

HONOURABLE MENTIONS:

Mayo footballer Andy Moran, Armagh footballer Jamie Clarke, Limerick hurler Séamus Hickey, Armagh footballer Ciaran McKeever, Down footballers past and present.

What a Shower!

Ireland is the greatest place in the world to be a sports fan, but there is one terrible drawback to attending sporting events in this country: the bleedin' rain. Met Éireann claims it rains 193 days of the year at Belmullet – but we know things are far worse than that. Luckily, years of being soaked at matches have turned us into MacGyver where dryness is concerned. Give us a Tayto wrapper, a match programme and a shoelace, and we'll make you a hurricane-proof rain jacket.

The match programme, as all GAA fans know, has two functions: one as a source of information, the other as rain protection. As this fan at the 2002 hurling final found out, the All-Ireland programme is so big it can cover the entire head and keep the sun out of your eyes. We can't explain the glumness of this man at a Donegal-Kerry match in Croker, but it looks like he'd prefer an umbrella.

Not even Houdini could extract himself from the knot that this Roscommon woman entangled herself in.

The GAA have an arcane rule that every county must employ one steward whose sole responsibility it is to dry the benches ahead of team photographs. Leitrim's James Glancy narrowly avoided landing himself in a puddle ahead of a Connacht championship game in 2011.

You've got to love the umbrella politics at work in this family, photographed at a Monaghan-Wexford qualifier back in 2006. It's clear that the older you are, the more entitled you are to dryness.

A passion for rain is engendered in the young. It's encouraging to see this mini Munster fan taking the healthy option of rain instead of a fizzy drink.

Who needs umbrellas, hats or even match programmes? This guy at the 2010 All-Ireland football quarter-finals kept himself dry with some aluminium foil that he found in his pocket. Pure genius.

Here are two men – one at Cheltenham, the other at a Waterford-Limerick game – who visibly the regret the decision not to purchase the match pro-gramme. It's a scientific fact that it is ten times more rain-resistant than the simple handkerchief.

It's not just fans and players who have to deal with squalls. Refs and umpires, too, are left defenceless when the rain comes. Try as he may, this umpire cannot disappear into his lab coat during a downfall that interrupted a Dublin-Westmeath hurling match.

A dry towel can be a hurler's best friend. That said, we have no idea why Antrim goalie Ryan McGarry thought draping himself in a towel would help him keep shots out of the net too.

Down with This Sort Of Thing

How to Stage an Irish Sports Protest

Compared to our bailed-out brethren in Greece and Spain, the Irish aren't exactly famous for protesting – strange, because when it comes to sport, we love nothing more than making a ridiculous sign and publicly airing our grievances. Enjoy some of the greatest examples of the Irish sporting protestor at work down through the years.

Decades of dithering by the FAI over their ground and the general mismanagement of their club ensured that Shamrock Rovers fans were always on the march. In 1987, members of KRAM (Keep Rovers at Milltown) took to the pitch after the last game at Glenmalure Park to voice their concerns about the club's future. And seventeen years later, there was this protest by Rovers fans ahead of a match against Derry City at Richmond Park, where they spray-painted messages on bin liners and wielded fake red cards. (A fake red card is an essential prop in any sports protest.)

No sports protest was more effective that the spontaneous action taken by Offaly fans in 1998, after the final whistle was blown a few minutes too early in their All-Ireland semi-final against Clare. Before Occupy Wall Street, there was Occupy Croker.

The Garth Brooks farce of summer 2014 remains one of the sorrier episodes in Ireland's history. The build-up to the 2014 Leinster hurling final was marred by this peaceful protest, in which fans attempted to save the cancelled gigs. Thankfully it proved futile.

Since Saipan nearly provoked a second civil war, it's no surprise that a buoyant protest movement was galvanised in the days after Roy Keane packed his bags and headed home to Cheshire to walk Triggs. This is our favourite sign from a peaceful pro-Keano rally outside the FAI's old offices in Merrion Square. This protester is so convinced of her message that she even brought an umbrella to protect her sign.

One of the most extreme Irish sporting protests was Dundalk United fan Maxi McAllister's 'happening' at the old FAI HQ in 2006. McAllister arrived in Merrion Square and demanded a meeting with the FAI chief executive and the Dundalk manager, after an independent group granted another club a place in the League of Ireland Premier Division. McAllister doused himself and the Christmas tree seen here in petrol. Thankfully no one was hurt, though McAllister would serve four months in prison.

Perhaps the only good thing to come out of the IRFU's mooted plan to deprofessionalise Connacht rugby in the early noughties was the protest movement it inspired. Here's a couple of the brilliant signs that helped to save the club. (Again, note fake red card.)

The
Wes Hoolahan
Hall of Fame

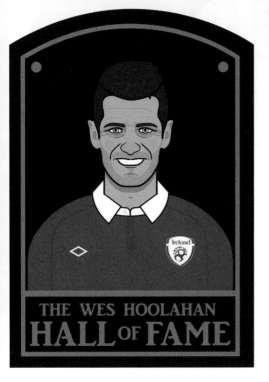

THE WES HOOLAHAN
HALL OF FAME

Irish sports fans love a victim. The Wes Hoolahan Hall of Fame is a non-profit organisation set up to honour the players whose esteem in the hearts of the public and media increased in direction proportion to the time they spent *not* playing. Some athletes make their fame off the field; these men became legends by not playing at all.

WES HOOLAHAN

Weso has his name above the door not because he was the first man to be criminally overlooked by an Ireland manager, but because no one has had their cause celebrated more passionately than this diminutive Dubliner.

Many factors contribute to Weso's mythical status: his storied underage career with Belvedere, his role in Shelbourne's glory years, and most importantly, his treatment during the Trapattoni era, which still causes existential tumult to Ireland fans. While Paul Green was anchoring the Ireland midfield, Weso was a pariah – and all the better for it.

Martin O'Neill has embraced Hoolahan's genius, even if he belittles Wes by saying he only plays well at the Aviva. Wes's role in Ireland's stirring second-half comeback against Poland in March 2015 inspired orgasmic reactions, especially by Giles and Dunphy.

ANDY REID

For a time there in 2009, it felt like Andy Reid was in with a shout of being nominated for the Ballon d'Or. The longer he went without playing for Ireland, the more his reputation grew. By sidelining Reid, Trapattoni ensured that the midfielder would remain a darling of the Irish supporters for all time.

O'Neill picked Reid in his first friendlies as Ireland boss. This was done mostly to court the sympathies of the Irish public. These days, Reid is a long way from the Ireland team, and no one seems too bothered.

GEORDAN MURPHY

Geordan Murphy was the stick used to beat Eddie O'Sullivan for years. Here was proof of Eddie's dour conservatism and pathological inflexibility. It started going wrong in the early days. Murphy was a bit 'out of sight, out of mind' over at Leicester and so was overlooked by the Irish setup in the early 2000s. Eddie persisted in picking Girvan Dempsey, a man often patronised as a safe pair of hands.

After his reign ended and his apologia was published, O'Sullivan was regularly asked to account for his refusal to play Geordan. The bemused ex-manager acknowledged that Murphy was a fantastically talented player but maintained that he had flaws in his game.

DAVID O'LEARY

The Icelandic Triangular Tournament in 1986 was not only the first tournament we ever won, but also the trigger for one of the longest player-manager stand-offs in Irish football.

David O'Leary's position was that he couldn't be arsed cancelling a family holiday to play in a meaningless competition after a long season. Jack Charlton wasn't impressed and never forgave him. Jack proceeded to pick the much inferior Mick McCarthy for the next five years, relegating O'Leary to the bench – at best. O'Leary became a cause célèbre for the RTÉ panel, particularly Dunphy, in the early Charlton years.

IAN MADIGAN

During the 2013 Six Nations, Madigan became Declan Kidney's Geordan Murphy; a player whose outrageous flair petrified an inherently conservative coach. Ahead of the Scotland game, Kidney faced a dilemma: Sexton was crocked, and he had lost faith in an ageing Ronan O'Gara. Kidney decided to take a wild punt on his starting outhalf – not on the golden boy of the Leinster academy, though, but on Ulster's 21-year-old-but-17-year-old-looking Paddy Jackson.

Of course, Kidney wasn't the only coach to doubt Madigan's tactical nous at out-half. Matt O'Connor was definitely Team Gopperth while the Kiwi was knocking about the RDS. And Joe Schmidt's selection of Ian Keatley ahead of Madigan in the 2015 Six Nations curtain-raiser against Italy suggests that maybe Kidney was on to something all along.

69

JAMES MCCLEAN

When McClean made his debut as a substitute in the Ireland–Czech Republic pre-Euro 2012 friendly, the deafening roar and standing ovation that greeted the Derryman stunned Trapattoni. His voice croaking with frustration, Trap later remarked to the press corps, 'I thought: "Is Messi or Maradona or Pelé coming on?"'

McClean subsequently became a fixture on the Irish team, but once defenders figured him out, it quickly transpired that he wasn't the messiah. It turned out that he had just been a player on the crest of a wave in the first few months of 2012. His second season with Sunderland was a disaster, and he wasn't to remain a Premier League player for much longer.

TONY WARD

Limerick babe magnet Tony Ward was the original Weso of Irish sport. Despite being a European Rugby Player of the Year, Ward was overlooked by the Irish selection committee ahead of our test match with Australia in 1979. Ollie Campbell started at outhalf, and Ireland beat Australia in both tests. Campbell then steered Ireland to the Five Nations championship in 1982. It's difficult not to accept that the right call was made, but Ward maintained vigorous support in the press and on the terraces. Eamon Dunphy – chief booster of Wesos everywhere – dabbled in a spot of rugby writing upon Ward's retirement in 1987. He opined that Ward had been 'the victim of bigotry, snobbishness and hypocrisy that is unique to rugby union'.

The Reel
Ould Times

Ireland's Goldenest (+ Shitest) Years

Winston Churchill said that 'history is written by the victors'. He was wrong. In our time, in our land, history is written by the producers of *Reeling in the Years*. How our perceptions of momentous years of Irish history – 1690, 1847, 1916 – might change if they could be re-experienced through half-hour TV reels. We hereby present to you the three best and the three worst years of recent Irish history, based on a forensic watch of Ireland's greatest nostalgia kick.

THE GOLDENEST YEARS IN IRISH HISTORY

3. 2004

Ireland held the EU presidency and was roundly praised. Half the multinationals in America arrived, as did the Eastern Europeans, and emigration dipped to record lows. Future FG backbencher and RTÉ agriculture correspondent George Lee was predicting a bright future for the country. On a sombre note, the auld lads in rural Ireland were shafted by the introduction of the smoking ban.

The Olympics (Waterford Crystal and all that) were shite, as were both All-Ireland finals, but Ireland claimed its first Triple Crown in nineteen years. This classically portentous episode of *RITY* ends with Seamus Heaney reading poetry at an EU event in Farmleigh. You can almost hear Eamon Dunphy snorting about 'Official Ireland'.

2007

The high-water mark of Irish decadence. We were still in that dreamlike state of boom-time. Bertie Ahern was the Mr. Big of Irish politics, and Fine Gael – not Fianna Fáil – were trying to keep the tribunal allegations out of the news. Despite what that looper Morgan Kelly was saying, we were preparing for a soft landing.

In sport, the Irish football team plunged to new depths, but we had Pádraig Harrington winning the Open, David Gillick taking gold at the European indoors, and John Hayes weeping during the national anthem before Ireland hammered England in Croke Park. (The producers wisely omitted the woeful Rugby World Cup, but of course TV3 aired that.)

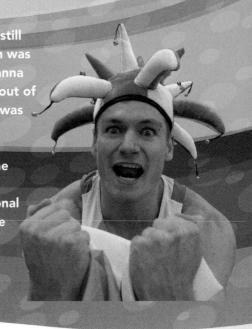

1994

Going by *RITY*, these were the greatest twelve months in Irish history. Despite shocking tragedies, such as the Loughinisland Massacre, this was the year when centuries of misery turned around. We had the IRA ceasefire, Riverdance, Ireland beating Italy in the Giants Stadium, Simon Geoghegan's try in Twickenham, and Sonia O'Sullivan taking gold in Helsinki.

With the 1980s – a long tale of misery, emigration and heaves against Charlie Haughey – now well behind us, we were seeing the first baby steps of the Celtic Tiger.

The episode finishes with a rousing rendition of 'Here Come the Good Times' by A House. Only Limerick people watch it and feel melancholic.

CLOSE RUN THING:
1990 (Italia '90, Mary Robinson, pound coins, Nelson Mandela, Brian Keenan).

3.

1981

The year Bob Geldof's alternative national anthem, 'Banana Republic', topped the charts. 1981 was dominated by hunger strikes, riots, the appalling Stardust fire and Charlie Haughey bounding around the country kissing cheeks and talking shite.

In sport, the Irish rugby team sparked protests when they decided to tour South Africa. Their wooden spoon win didn't even make the final cut of *RITY*.

2.

2008

The year the Irish economy collapsed. The *Reeling in the Years* producers dutifully obliged with plenty of shots of panicky *Wolf of Wall Street* types screaming into their telephones in their IFSC bunkers. The government decided to 'rescue' the economy by guaranteeing the banks. Inspirational taoiseach Brian Cowen was front and centre defending the move.

On the bright side, future Fine Gael councillor Kenneth Egan won silver in Beijing and returned to Clondalkin as a hero.

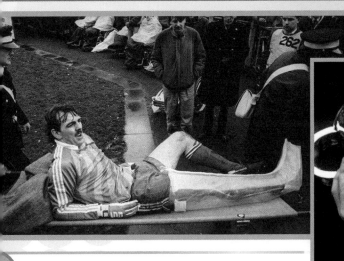

1986

RITY: 1986 is one of the most unremittingly bleak half hours of Irish TV ever produced. It begins with Ian Paisley bellowing about Dublin rule and only goes downhill from there. Violence up north, strikes, floods, Brian Keenan's kidnapping, Simply Red – the woe goes on and on.

The episode finishes with Mary Black warbling 'As I Leave Behind Neidin' while a load of sheepish-looking young lads tell Tommie Gorman there's nothing for them here and they're fecking off to London. To top it off, there's an extended clip of Chris de Burgh singing 'Lady In Red'.

CLOSE RUN THING:
1984 (Dunnes strike, IRA bombings, heroin, Indian chemical leaks, Ethiopian famine).

How to Pose for an

Irish Sports

Photo Shoot

Advertisers love Irish sportspeople. They are, after all, some of the most trusted and beloved folk on this island. But a sports star's good name alone will not sell a product; it takes an image to properly seduce the consumer. And in some cases, apparently it takes an image of a well-known sporting personality beside a scantily clad model. Here we explain the rules, highlight the true stars, and present some of the most epic examples of the Irish photo shoot from over the years.

RATIOS

First rule of an Irish sports photo shoot: if the star-to-model ratio is 2:1 or greater, the model must be carried like *this*.

Peter Clohessy masks are, as ever, optional.

When the star-to-model ratio is even, the model must be carried like *this*.

A young Paul O'Connell, when outnumbered by models, realises his best bet is to wear a rugby jersey with slacks.

77

WEAPONRY

When you're struggling to sell or promote an item, keep in mind that there's nothing quite as persuasive as the threat of antiperspirant force. Here, Seán Óg and Rocky Elsom roar in fear at the sight of this deodorant-wielding commando.

Two League of Ireland players driving a tank?! OK, it's not the scariest prospect in the world, but a tank is a tank.

OVERSIZED ACCESSORIES

Next rule of the Irish sports photoshoot: as the accessories get bigger, the models' clothes get skimpier.

Trap mightn't have the eyesight of a twenty-year-old, but this phone seems totally impractical. How would he get it in his pocket?

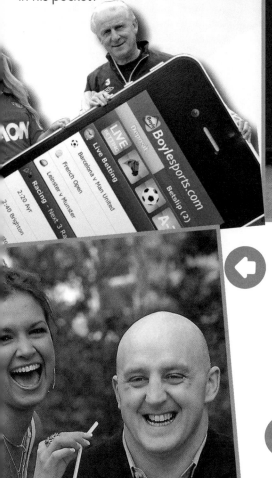

Honey I blew up the tennis racquet.

We can't be sure what Keith Wood is promoting here, but he has managed to discover the world's largest glass of Baileys.

Meanwhile, the world's largest crisp bag made an appearance back when Hunky Dorys announced its sponsorship of Drogheda United's ground. There are still only around four crisps in that bag.

79

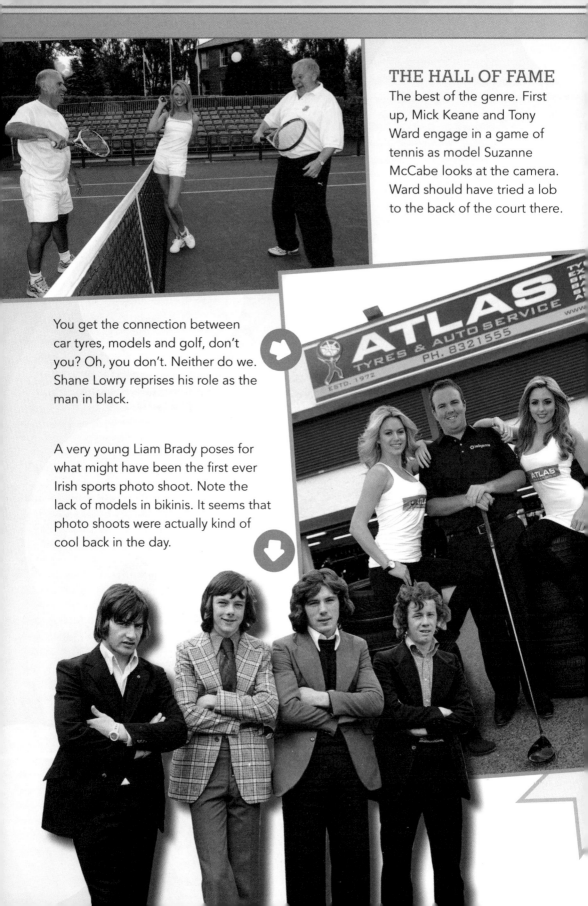

THE HALL OF FAME

The best of the genre. First up, Mick Keane and Tony Ward engage in a game of tennis as model Suzanne McCabe looks at the camera. Ward should have tried a lob to the back of the court there.

You get the connection between car tyres, models and golf, don't you? Oh, you don't. Neither do we. Shane Lowry reprises his role as the man in black.

A very young Liam Brady poses for what might have been the first ever Irish sports photo shoot. Note the lack of models in bikinis. It seems that photo shoots were actually kind of cool back in the day.

Taken in 2010, there's a definite retro feel here that harkens back to the black and white days of the Irish sports photo shoot. We've got Sam Allardyce, Frank Stapleton and a model/pilot at Dublin Airport with a Mac laptop and a football. It shouldn't work, but somehow it does – largely due to Big Sam's kick-and-stare-deathly-into-the-camera approach.

Paging Dr O'Shea. Paging Dr O'Shea. John O'Shea was the first Irish footballer to be signed up to promote the stethoscope industry. Stethoscope sales in Ireland skyrocketed after this campaign.

CHRISTY O'CONNOR
THE CLUB

WINNER

The Club is a book about life, death and hurling in Clare. And nothing says 'life, death and hurling in Clare' like a model in a Doora-Barefield jersey and hot pants.

DOORA-BAREFIELD

81

Once upon a time, there was a Dave Kearney who lived in a pink stiletto. Munster fans point to this photo and say, 'This is what we're talking about.'

There's nothing an Irishman finds sexier than a woman in a GAA jersey. But a woman who wears a GAA jersey and works at a building site? That's obscene.

Ray Houghton trying to get Toto Schillaci fat on Cornettos. Too little, too late, Ray!

Every now and then, models are asked to take part in sports photo shoots without a sports personality present. The results can vary. Here Dublin's Ruth O'Neill makes one of the worst attempts at catching a ball we've ever seen.

Irish models are more than just pretty faces. Some possess magical powers, like this woman who can turn men's heads into rugby balls.

One of Brian O'Driscoll's early forays into the property market goes awry when a tag rugby game involving giant-sized models runs riot on Sandymount Strand.

This sports broadcast goes horribly wrong when Des Curran superglues a football to Nadia Forde's head.

83

ALL-TIME GREATS: MICHAEL RING

Never has any Irish politician shown as much attention to his brief as Minister of State for Sport Michael Ring, TD. It's clear that Ring not only sees himself as the Minister of State for Sport but also as the Minister of State for Sports Photo Shoots. Here, he brings his hurling skills to the Aviva. No photo shoot is complete without Mr Ring playing keepie-uppies with a hurley and sliotar.

Clearly Mr Ring was not chosen for the job because of his sports skills. Stephanie Roche looks particularly disappointed by his effort to replicate her Puskás-nominated goal.

Even in a suit and loafers, the Junior Minister can beat kids half his age at the 1500 metres. Here he renews his running rivalry with Enda Kenny, which dates back to the 1970s, when they were Ógra FG's most talented long-distance runners.

Mr Ring's true passion is boxing. In this photo, he and his gold-medal winning sparring partner prep for the annual Fine Gael vs Fianna Fáil white-knuckle boxing series on the Dáil plinth.

ALL-TIME GREATS: TRAP

In his five years managing Ireland, Giovanni Trapattoni took part in a record-breaking number of photo shoots. He was a different man when the camera was on him: his poor English was no longer an obstacle, and his suave-but-goofy septuagenarian vibe was complemented perfectly by the young ladies. In his wake, he left a photo shoot void.

Louise Kavanagh is joyful in the presence of two legends of football. Trap made sure to ask the wax Jack to let him do the talking.

Even after Irish fans turned their backs on Trap and the crap tactics he forced upon us, Ireland's models stood by their man.

Less enjoyable for Trap were his football tutorials with Mr Tayto.

The Amazing Technicolour Cult
of the Irish Football
Piggyback

Centuries from now, when robot anthropologists try to get their tin heads around the strange rituals of Irish sportspeople, one single pastime will separate our country's footballers from their rugby and GAA-playing brethren: the joyful piggyback.

KEANO

(1) The Irish training piggyback seems to have started in 1996 with Alan McLoughlin giving Roy Keane a rest from training. The normally dour Keano was never happier than when he was on one of his teammates' backs. (2) Two years later, Roy has trimmed his mop but is as cheery as ever as he forms an alternative goalkeeping team with future broadband salesman Discopants Quinn. (3) Keane was not only a taker of piggybacks: he was equally happy to ferry players about. Just ask Gary Breen. (4) To think all of the heartache of Saipan could have been avoided if Keane had just spent the rest of the training camp on the back of Andy O'Brien.

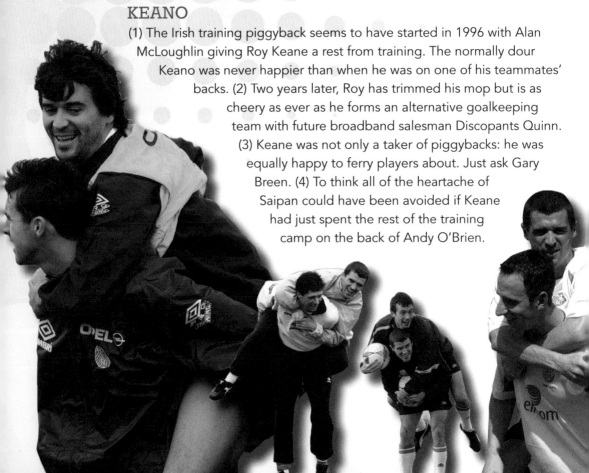

BIG DOTS

Leaving aside his god-given goal-scoring ability, Gary Doherty was essential to early-noughties Ireland squads because of his natural piggyback-giving attributes. He even worked as a human rickshaw on his J1 in San Diego. Stephen McPhail was always first in the queue for a Doherty-back.

CARR

As a defender, Stephen Carr raged against the machine. But off the field, he was never as content as when he was taxiing David Connolly back and forth to the team hotel.

DOUGLAS

Jonathan Douglas knew the best way to get over being dropped was to get as close to Joe Murphy as he could.

SUPER MICK

Mick McCarthy was so glad that his revolutionary training method had been successful that he let Stan in on the secret, just in case he should ever have to control his own team of internationals.

STAN

An innovator in his playing days and his management career, Steve Staunton here attempts football's first-ever three-man piggyback in conjunction with Kevin Kilbane and Jason McAteer.

QUINNY

Niall Quinn had the longest back in the history of Irish football and thus was a legend of the piggyback. Here, as Stephen Carr struggles with Rory Delap, David Connolly exalts on the back of the Quinnasaurus.

Holy Sliotar!

Fifty years ago, the Church's hold over Irish society was all-encompassing. Back when the idea of having a manager was somewhat foreign, it was, in many cases, priests who served as the real tactical innovators of Gaelic games.

Maybe it's no surprise that priests were successful as managers: it's sinful for a player to question your authority, homilies are great practice for team talks, and there's plenty of downtime between masses to ponder tactics. Below you'll find the Balls.ie list of the Top 5 GAA Priests of All Time.

FATHER KEVIN FAY

The long-time manager of St Pat's of Cavan, Fay is best known for his exuberant celebration after managing his college to victory in the Rannafast Cup in 2012. In compliance with the edicts laid down by Vatican II, he is known to say ultra-quick masses on the days Cavan have Championship games.

FATHER TOM FOGARTY

A former Tipperary hurler in his seminary days, Fogarty managed Tipp in the mid-1990s and Offaly from 2001 to 2002. Neither spell was especially successful; he took over a Tipperary team in a time of transition and an Offaly team in outright decline. In both of his seasons in charge of Tipp, they beat Waterford only to be pipped by Limerick – once after a replay in the '96 Munster final. In 2006, he guided Tipperary to the U21 Munster title, and they were narrowly beaten by Kilkenny in the All-Ireland final replay.

FATHER HARRY BOHAN

Father Harry sparked a revival of Clare hurling when he shepherded the Banner to two National League titles in the 1970s. He returned in the early noughties as a selector with Anthony Daly. In 2006, he became enmeshed in a strange and unholy row with his spiritual protégé Ger Loughnane. Feakle's finest was apoplectic that Father Harry – and not he – had been selected for an award for 'special services to Clare hurling'. Depending on your attitude towards Loughnane, the dispute either enhanced or diminished Father Harry's saintly reputation.

CANON MICHAEL O'BRIEN

In the summer of 1990, Babs Keating was asked about Cork's chances against his Tipp team, who were defending All-Ireland hurling champs. Keating remarked that 'donkeys don't win derbies'. Cork manager Canon Michael O'Brien took note. He had already managed Cork to Liam MacCarthy in 1984 and coached UCC to eight Fitzgibbon Cups during the 1980s. Needless to say, O'Brien's donkeys not only beat Tipp in Thurles that July but also beat Galway in the All-Ireland that September in a surreal goal-fest.

FATHER TOMMY MAHER

Brian Cody's mentor, Maher coached the Kilkenny hurlers from the late 1950s to the late 1970s. It was the Cats' greatest era – that is, until Cody himself took the reins. Maher died in March 2015 and is remembered as a godfather of modern hurling. He believed that 'the only tactic is technique' and encouraged passing, both from the hand and the hurl. In an era when backs used to just leather the ball forward, Maher preached that no ball should be sent in without a recipient in mind. An early prototype of Dónal O'Grady.

8 Things We Can't Believe Actually Happened in Irish Sport

LAR AND THE QUEEN

Forget sipping Guinness or dropping a cúpla focal at a dinner party – the most important thing Queen Elizabeth accomplished during her historic visit to Ireland in 2011 was to shake the hand of Tipp's Lar Corbett in the Hogan Stand dressing rooms in Croker.

MICK O'DWYER KIDNAPPED

In the run-up to the 2007 Hillbilly Tractor Run in aid of special-needs charity KARE, someone in Wicklow had this idea: let's pretend to kidnap Mick O'Dwyer to generate some publicity for the event. That's no way to treat a GAA legend.

CHINESE HURLING IN CROKER

It's obligatory that any male foreign dignitary visiting our shores must pose for the cameras with a hurl in his hand. When the vice-president of China, Xi Jinping – who would become president a year later – came to Ireland in 2012, his handlers insisted he go the whole hog and have a cut at scoring a point into the Hill. Safe to say his one-hand grip never really caught on.

THE LADS ON TOUR

Ah, they were innocent times, weren't they? Not many Ireland fans could afford the flight to Tehran to watch the second leg of Ireland's 2002 World Cup qualifier with Iran. Two people who could were future billionaire Denis O'Brien and F1 legend Eddie Jordan. By the photographic evidence here, they enjoyed themselves in the terraces with Davy Keogh.

DAVY KEOGH SAYS HELLO

HILL 16 WAS BLESSED

The redevelopment of Croke Park finished ahead of the 2005 Championship, and it would have been sacrilege to reopen the stadium without the blessing of a higher power. So a few days before St Patrick's Day, Dr Dermot Clifford, Archbishop of Cashel & Emly and patron of the GAA, along with Bertie Ahern and the Lord Mayor of Dublin, gathered on the Hill to consecrate the ground.

CHARLIE AND THE DUBS

The 1983 All-Ireland football semi-final was notable for a few reasons. It was held in Cork, for one thing, after the Rebels drew with the Dubs in Croker. When the Dubs eventually won the replay, opposition leader Charles J Haughey was among the fans in Páirc Uí Chaoimh leading the jubilant celebrations. The Dubs would go on to play, and beat, Galway in the final that year.

THE MICHAEL LOWRY HOSPITALITY SUITE

We love this photograph of Michael Lowry in 1997, lording it up on his own at Semple Stadium. If Semple did corporate boxes, they'd look a lot like this.

MCCREEVEY'S FIFTEEN

Here we see Charlie McCreevey picking the Kildare team for the 1998 All-Ireland final. OK, this may never have happened, but he did have the bantz with Glen Ryan at the media night ahead of the 1998 All-Ireland final. That's some Kildare corsage he's wearing.

Are you a Football Hipster?

The massive reaction back in 2013 to the Balls.ie '25 Steps to Becoming a Football Hipster' spoke of a hardcore who were happy to poke gentle fun at themselves.

Since then, inevitably, it has become very un-hipster to write about football hipsters. But they're still out there. And, scariest of all, you might be one.

1. You only own football jerseys that make some kind of statement. Your vintage Parma jersey might be a statement of solidarity with a club in financial peril. Your 1970s Dutch kit might be a statement about collectivism. Your Rooney #10 Man United kit might be a nod to normcore. It's all fine; there's a reason.

2. You buy *La Gazzetta dello Sport* whenever you get the chance. Google Translate has nothing on the feeling of those pink pages in your fingertips. *Gazzetta* also remains the standard by which player ratings will be measured. After all, they were giving Michael Carrick 8/10 as far back as 2009.

9. You were secretly glad when the 2014 World Cup tightened up as the group stages ended and the tense, taut golden goal nature of knockout began.

10. You consistently pour scorn on the Premier League. You say it's *Hawaii Five-O* to the Bundesliga's *The Wire*. You say it has utterly lost the art of defending, and that the perfect game ends 0-0.

'REEEBER Y BOCA'

11. You wonder aloud what Gianni Brera would make of today's football media.

12. You snicker in annoyance anytime a manager bemoans the fact that he will lose a player to the Africa Cup of Nations.

13. You voted for van Persie for the 2014 Puskás award.

14. You believe Louis van Gaal is the great

3. You still insist that James Richardson is a god. You call him 'AC Jimbo' and endure an hour of Fletch and Sav on BT Sport just because they cut to James at a coffee table reading continental papers.

4. You have a monthly magazine budget of at least €15. That will cover *Four-FourTwo* and *WorldSoccer*. You smile every time *WorldSoccer* feature a Brian Glanville column, and you frown every time you remember that *FourFourTwo* finished the secret player column.

5. Speaking of football periodicals, if, for some ridiculous reason, you don't have a *Blizzard* subscription – get one. Also track down Issue Zero and give it pride of place on your shelf.

6. You were into Zonal Marking back when it was man to man.

7. Reading *Inverting the Pyramid* changed your life; you still harbour dreams of a UEFA badge.

8. You dismiss all heat maps.

influencer of our age and has won the ideological battle with Johan Cruyff over how the game should be played. He achieved this by submitting to reason and (pause for effect) realising Holland must play 3-5-2 at the World Cup while watching his great foe Ronald Koeman's Feyenoord's team. Note the irony.

15. You feel spasms of uncomfortable joy whenever you read Barney Ronay's lyrical flourishes about tactical innovations.

16. You have no interest in the Ballon d'Or.

17. You believe Marcelo Bielsa is the heir to Valeriy Lobanovskyi and your ideal football coach.

18. You hype up South American derbies like they are the biggest games in the world. You tell everyone you cannot believe people are looking forward to Super Sunday on Sky

when it's only six hours until River and Boca play.

19. You are well aware of the difference between a 'proactive' and a 'reactive' coach.

'PAREEE-SAN-JYRMAH'

20. You harbour a secret crush on Sam Allardyce.

21. You endured the fall of Borussia Dortmund honourably. The end of the Klopp reign has been very tough for you to take, but you saw it coming the moment Arjen

21

0

Robben scampered clear and scored the winner in the 2013 CL final.

22. You're concerned that Jürgen Klopp's method of playing will mean he will only ever stay three or four years at a club.

23. You believe that *Revista de la Liga* have lost something since they got rid of Mark Bolton, but you like their new set.

24. You religiously tune in to BT Sport's European football show and applaud the station for putting journalists on panels.

'GHEL-SIN-KIR-SSSHHHHHH-HEN'

25. Your Irish footballing messiah is not Wes Hoolahan; Glenn Whelan is much more important.

26. You sigh anytime you hear the words 'maverick' and 'Zlatan Ibrahimović' in the same sentence.

27. You've read *The Miracle of Castel Di Sangro* more than once.

28. You only pronounce team names in the language of the country they're from. So it's 'Reeeber y Boca' in the 'Bombanerrrrrrro', 'Pareee-san-jyr-mah' and Ireland's Euro '88

game was in 'Ghel-sin-kirssshhhhhh-en'.

29. You have had Martin Ødegaard on your radar since he was eleven.

30. You remind everyone that Sacchi's Milan were the pioneers of pressing.

31. You live-tweet the *Sunday Supplement*, pointing out why it's silly with every sentence.

32. You were in full agreement with Roy Hodgson's pick of Javier Mascherano as the player of the 2014 World Cup.

33. You're considering learning a second language but can't decide which one. French would let you read *France Football*, but Portuguese would let you read Tim Vickery's Copa Libertadores posts on Brazilian websites.

34. You are comforted by the relatively poor scoring ratio of Leo Messi and Cristiano Ronaldo at international football tournaments. It is a monument to the collective.

25

35. YOU IGNORE THE PREVIOUS THIRTY-FOUR STEPS AND INSTEAD TO CHOOSE TO TRAVEL HOME AND AWAY WITH A LEAGUE OF IRELAND TEAM.

26

2

A Great Bunch of Lads

Father Ted Power Rankings

We all recognise *Father Ted* as the greatest piece of art that Ireland has produced in the last fifty years. For the sake of posterity, we think it's necessary to have a list of every priest to appear on the programme during its three-season run. Though they may all be equal in God's eyes, some priests are just better than other priests.

1. FATHER TED CRILLY

Parish priest on Craggy Island. He left his old post in Wexford due to uproar when he absconded to Las Vegas with the cash raised to send a sick child to Lourdes. Consistently claims that the money was just resting in his account. One-time winner of the Golden Cleric Award. Not a racist. SAYS: 'FASCISTS DRESS IN BLACK AND GO AROUND TELLING PEOPLE WHAT TO DO, WHEREAS PRIESTS ...'

2. FATHER DOUGAL MCGUIRE

Ended up on Craggy Island after an incident in Black-rock that 'irreparably damaged' a group of nuns. Doesn't believe in an afterlife, struggles with his faith and thinks the Vatican is an art gallery. He loves the Eurovision, rollerblading, *Byker Grove* and eggs, and he may be an AC Milan fan.
SAYS: 'TED, YOU'RE NOT GOING TO BELIEVE THIS! CLINT EASTWOOD HAS BEEN ARRESTED FOR A CRIME HE DIDN'T – OH WAIT, NO, IT'S A FILM.'

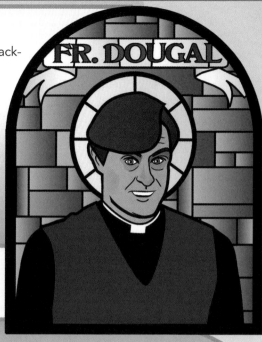

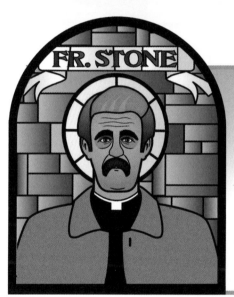

3. FATHER PAUL STONE

Priest/amateur artist who goes on his holidays to Craggy Island every year. A friend of Father Jim Doogan's, but he adores Father Ted even more. Survived a near-fatal lightning strike in 1995. His brother is a doctor, which may contribute to the tension between Father Stone and his dad. Hasn't talked to Father Shortall in quite some time.
SAYS: 'NO THANKS, I'M FINE.'

4. FATHER NOEL FURLONG

Headed the St Luke's Youth Group before they fled to Paraguay. Father Noel is a congenial sort, but his boundless energy can be irritating. He really likes Tony and Queen and is friends with Father Sweeney, who has a bladder the size of a Terry's Chocolate Orange. He once met Chris Evans, but only briefly.
SAYS: 'HERE'S TONY'S PARENTS WHEN THEY HEAR THAT I'VE EATEN TONY: "WHY DID YOU EAT TONY? TONY WAS OUR ONLY SON!"'

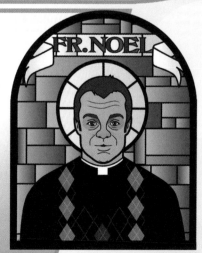

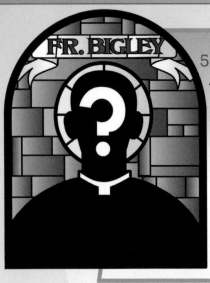

FR. BIGLEY

5. FATHER BIGLEY

Attended the same seminary as Father Ted, where the pair used to sneak out to Dana concerts. After being ordained, he befriended a priest who was sending arms to Iraq and said mass at OJ Simpson's wedding. He has terrible blotches and puffy fish lips bigger than the rest of his face.

TED: 'FATHER BIGLEY LISTENS TO DANA AND HE'S NOT MAD.'

DOUGAL: 'WHY'S HE IN THAT HOME THEN?'

TED: 'HE'S IN THAT HOME BECAUSE ... BECAUSE OF THOSE FIRES.'

6. Father Jack
7. Father Dick Byrne
8. Bishop Len Brennan
9. Father Larry Duff
10. Father Austin Purcell
11. Father Damo Lennon
12. Father Barty Dunne
13. Father Fintan Stack
14. Father Todd Unctious
15. Father Billy O'Dwyer
16. Father Cyril MacDuff
17. Father Fay
18. Father Cullen
19. Father Romeo Sensini
20. Father Jose Fernandez
21. Bishop Tom McCaskell
22. Father Kevin
23. Father Jessup
24. Father Liam Deliverance
25. Father Derek Beeching
26. Father Clarke
27. Father Joe Briefly
28. Father Liam Finnegan
29. Father Seamus Fitzpatrick
30. Father Harry Coyle
31. Father Ben
32. Father 'Frosty' Frost
33. Father Benny Cake
34. The posh priest
35. Bishop Facks
36. Father Walton
37. Father Ned Fitzmaurice
38. Father Shortall
39. Father Niall Haverty
40. Father Buzz Cagney
41. Father Terry

'COWBOYS, TED. THEY'RE A BUNCH OF COWBOYS!'

FATHER LIAM DELIVERANCE

'OASIS OR BLUR?'
FATHER DAMO LENNON

42. Father Cleary
43. Father Billy
44. Father Deegan
45. Father Reilly
46. Father Fitzgerald
47. Father Williams
48. Bishop Lindsay
49. Bishop Jordan
50. Bishop Eddie O'Neill
51. Father Shaft
52. Father Flynn
53. Father O'Shea
54. Father Cave
55. Father Nick
56. Father Windy Shepherd Henderson I
57. Father Rory
58. Father Ken
59. Father Paul Cleary
60. Father Tiernan
61. Father Rafter
62. Father Cafferty
63. Father Leonard
64. Father Gallagher
65. Father Jim Doogan

'YOU WILL ADDRESS ME BY MY PROPER TITLE, YOU LITTLE BOLLOCKS!'

BISHOP LEN BRENNAN

66. Father Jim Johnson
67. Father Clippett
68. Father Fitzgibbon
69. Father Carol
70. Father Jim Sutton
71. Father Clint Power
72. Father Alan
73. Father Brian Eno
74. Father Sweeney
75. Father Jimmy Ranable
76. Father Hegarty
77. Father Mackie
78. Father Nolan
79. Father Daly
80. Father Windy Shepherd Henderson II
81. Father Windy Shepherd Henderson III
82. Father O'Rourke
83. Father Tom Coogan
84. Father Burke
85. Father Windy Shepherd Henderson IV
86. Father Windy Shepherd Henderson V
87. Father Windy Shepherd Henderson VI
88. Drunk priest who blabs to Father Unctious

The Irish Sporting Mammy

Behind almost every successful sportsperson is a devoted mother. This is especially the case in Ireland. There would be none of the sporting delights we savour weekend after weekend without our mammies. It's not just the little things mammies do – the lifts to and from training, the carb-heavy meals, the endless loads of laundry – it's the self-belief they instil, and their constant devotion to our cause in the terraces.

In one of the nicer traditions in the Leinster Schools Cup – and maybe all Irish sport – the winning captain and losing captain at the Senior Cup final are presented with their trophies alongside their mothers. Here, Brian Glennon is pictured with his mother Una, reveling in all the southside 1985 pomp. (Some fur coat.) And in more recent times, Fergal Cleary's mam Marian provided a consoling shoulder after Clongowes lost the 2014 Senior Cup to Blackrock.

After Andy Lee shocked Matt Korobov to became WBO middle-weight champion in December 2014, who was the first person on the tarmac at Shannon Airport to greet him upon his homecoming? His mam, Anne.

Here's the country's most famous #13 stopping to celebrate with GOD – Geraldine O'Driscoll, that is – minutes after Ireland won the Championship in Stade de France in March 2014. The other two hands around Brian are those of his father, Frank. Truly, the first family of Irish sport.

John Mullane is the most passionate man in the history of hurling, so it should come as no surprise that he kisses his mother Kathleen with the same gusto with which he plays. This moment was captured after Waterford beat Cork in the 2007 Munster semi-final.

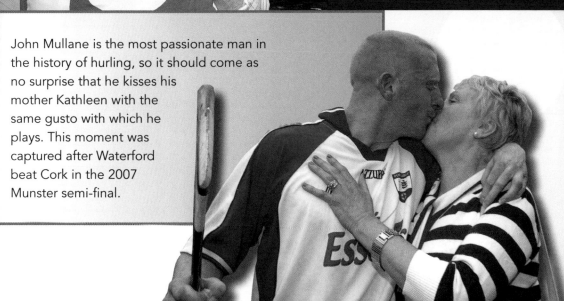

Mary O'Sullivan deserves our eternal praise for birthing and rearing Ireland's greatest ever athlete, her daughter Sonia. Here Mary and her other daughter Gillian enjoy a well-earned cup of tea as they await Sonia's appearance on the track at Sydney's Olympic Park in 2000.

After Shane Lowry won the 2009 Irish Open in a sudden-death playoff in the sodden twilight at Baltray, the first person he embraced was not fellow Offalyman and then-taoiseach Brian 'Biffo' Cowen, but his mother Bridget.

The mothers of Special Olympics athletes are some of the greatest people in the country. Here's Nichola Farrell, who played for the Irish Special Olympics basketball team, being comforted by her mother, Bernadette, after Team Ireland lost the gold medal game in the 2011 World Summer Games.

The Curious Case of the Irish Mascot

Irish sports teams have always been ambivalent about mascots. There was a long-held feeling that fans were above the sight of men in furry suits stalking our side-lines: we take our games too seriously for that kind of lark. There was of course Macul, Opel's Euro '88 wolfhound, but the reception towards him was indifferent.

As the Celtic Tiger took hold and Ireland became more Americanised, mascots started to appear at GAA matches in fits and starts. Counties faced an immediate roadblock: most GAA nicknames are just about impossible to anthropomorphise. How exactly do you represent a Tribesman or a Metropolitan or a Rebel in mascot form, let alone a Déise or a Bannerman?

The 2003 hurling championship saw the brief introduction of mascots in Kilkenny and Wexford. There's something adorable about this oversized dog wearing the Yellow Bellies' jersey and what seems to be a pair of boxer shorts. As for this Kilkenny cat, well, the less said the better. With a broad-brimmed black hat that your great-aunt might wear to wedding, it looks a bit like

the fifth Musketeer. We like to think that Brian Cody personally set that mascot suit ablaze during Kilkenny's All-Ireland celebrations that September.

The GAA got serious about mascots again in 2013, when they introduced Fionn, an Irish terrier, as their official mascot. According to the GAA website, he is 'used to communicate the GAA ethos and key messages'. We don't really know what kind of key messages a cuddly brown creature can communicate, but we're always amused by the sight of Fionn on All-Ireland day (right).

In rugby, meanwhile, it makes sense to have a mascot. They're common in most professional sports these days, and Irish rugby fans require some sort of entertainment when Celtic League/Magners League/Rabo Direct/Guinness Pro12 games inevitably fizzle out.

To that extent, this country has yet to produce a mascot with the ability and enthusiasm of Leinster's Leo the Lion. Leo has established himself as an integral part of the RDS experience. Who can forget his ingenious Halloween costume from 2010? Or the time he met future partner Leona

the Lioness? Even Brian O'Driscoll was happy to share some victory champagne with Leo after Leinster won the 2014 Pro12 championship (above, top).

During the height of the Eddie O'Sullivan era, the Irish team flirted with a mascot of their own. Broc the wolfhound (below) was given a run-out in 2005 before being erased from history.

One mascot is lord of the League of Ireland sidelines: Hooperman. The Shamrock Rovers mascot is a super-hero turned Hoops fan. Whether he's doing the Ice Bucket Challenge, riding a white horse, wrestling with the Bray mascot, Rocky, or yanking the FAI Cup away from his Sligo cousin Benny the Bull, Hooperman keeps it pretty real.

A Brief
History of Irish
Bandwagons

Everyone loves a winner, especially in a country where winners on the international stage are few and far between. That desire to get behind a champion – *any* champion – has left us watching some pretty odd sports over the last thirty years.

1987: CYCLING

In July 1987, Stephen Roche won the Tour de France weeks after winning the Giro, and in the blink of an eye, the Irish bandwagon movement had begun. Charlie Haughey was there with Roche at the Champs-Élysées, and 250,000 people lined the streets of Dublin to give him a hero's welcome. Victory felt great.

1988: THE IRISH FOOTBALL TEAM

A bandwagon like none before was born in the terraces of Neckarstadion in Stuttgart on 12 June 1988. We had beaten England 1-0 in our first game at an international tournament. The wagon that hitched itself to Jack Charlton's Ireland team during Euro '88 would have a massive role in shaping Irish consciousness over the next two decades. It even spawned the Celtic Tiger (if you believe David McWilliams.)

1996: MICHELLE SMITH

Who would have imagined it: an Irish person winning three golds and a bronze swimming at the Olympics. Those hours after Smith's first gold were euphoric. And in terms of medals won, she is still Ireland's greatest Olympian. But the Michelle Smith bandwagon remains a cautionary tale in the dangers of blindly supporting an athlete purely based on their success.

2004: CIAN O'CONNOR

The 2004 Olympics were terrible for Ireland. But just when all seemed lost, one man and his horse hurdled into our living rooms to save the day. Not many of us knew show jumping was an Olympic sport before Athens, but nonetheless we were glad for Cian and Waterford Crystal. All those summers watching the Dublin Horse Show were worth it during that tense final round that saw O'Connor secure gold – Ireland's only medal at those Olympics. The doping story that followed was a surreal chapter in Irish sports history, but at least we got Tommy Tiernan's Waterford Crystal routine out of it.

2004: SHELBOURNE

The League of Ireland will never reach the dizzying heights of August 2004 when Shelbourne nearly reached the group stages of the Champions League. Such was the interest in their tie with Spanish giants Deportivo de La Coruña that the home fixture had to be moved to Lansdowne Road. Over 22,000 people saw Shels hold Deportivo to a scoreless draw. They were less fortunate in the return leg, and everything for the club – and the league – has gone pretty terribly since.

2006: MUNSTER RUGBY

Who will ever forget those famous away days when the Red Army stormed grounds in France and England in their thousands to watch Gaillimh, the Claw, ROG, Paulie, Fla, the Bull, Strings and Wally pull off dour but unlikely victories in the Heineken Cup? Munster's players and fans took on a mythical status during the noughties. That Thomand Park is now half empty most of the time proves just how heaving the Munster bandwagon was a decade ago.

2008: EOIN RHEINISCH

His is a name that most Irish people can't spell or pronounce, but that doesn't mean he wasn't publicly beloved for a couple of hours during the Beijing Olympics.

Rheinish had us all fooled: he was the last man to qualify in the semi-finals and finals of the K1 event but was first out of the traps in the final, shocking the world with an incredible time that put him in the medal reckoning. As competitor after competitor was dismissed, the confused Irish public began to rally around 'Our Rhino'. Alas it wasn't to be, as a devastating fourth place banished the canoeing bandwagon to the dustbin of history.

2011: CRICKET

The first occupants of the Irish cricket bandwagon took their seats on St Patrick's Day 2007 when Ireland shocked Pakistan at the World Cup. Planning permission to massively extend the cricket bandwagon was approved four years later in the 2011 World Cup in India, when Ireland shocked England. Kevin O'Brien's century earned him a place in folklore beside Brian Boru, Jeremiah O'Donovan Rossa, Charles Stewart Parnell and Michael Collins.

2011: CONOR NILAND

Who hasn't watched the splendour of Wimbledon and thought, 'This tournament needs some Irish people'? For one day in 2011, SW19 turned green thanks to Conor Niland, after he beat Nikola Mektic to qualify for Wimbledon. The draw meant he would only have to beat journeyman Adrian Mannarino in the first round to earn the right to lose to Roger Federer. Niland lead 4-1 in the fifth set but couldn't get over the line. The tennis bandwagon has been stalled since.

2012: ANNALISE MURPHY

Four years after Eoin Rheinish's near-medal, the Irish bandwagon again gathered around an obscure watersport. We didn't know what the hell the Laser Radial was – and it sounded pretty dangerous – but the country wasn't long getting behind Rathfarnham's Annalise Murphy when she set sail for Olympic gold. Her heart-breaking fourth place left many wondering if the Irish are cursed on the water, but it guaranteed that we'll all be sailing buffs by the time Rio rolls around.

In GAA terms, you are where you're from. A Mayoman can't simply swap allegiances when Galway get good. An Offalywoman takes no joy in seeing Laois or Westmeath enjoy success on the field – it reminds her of her own county's inadequacies. Fate gives us our county stripes, and those are the ones we're stuck with. As such, the relative success of a county will govern its citizens' prevailing moods, and there are four clearly identifiable dispositions: just fine, thanks; sated by semi-recent glories; cursed; and patronised by the media and other supporters. Here is where things stand in 2015.

The Balls Map of GAA Sentiment

CONNAGHT

Galway: The hurling half of the county is still wondering what happened in 2012, but at least they have the footballers to fall back on.

Leitrim: Possibly the most patronised entity in Irish sport.

Mayo: As cursed as cursed can be.

Roscommon: Though some Roscommoners might be old enough to be sated by the 1944 All-Ireland, the county's footballers have been benignly patronised for years now.

Sligo: They play in Croker once every thirty summers. Like many of the most patronised counties, they almost beat Kerry once in a qualifier (2009 in Sligo's case).

MUNSTER

Clare: If this Clare team only manage one All-Ireland, it will be a great disappointment. And yet: 29 September 2013. The day remains fresh in the minds of all who saw it.

Cork: Just fine, thanks – although fretting the future.

Kerry: Just fine, thanks.

Limerick: Cursed(ish). The many successes of Munster rugby down through the years were fully enjoyed, but they paper over a void. The county desperately yearns for a breakthrough in hurling.

Tipperary: Brutal losses to Kilkenny aside, they're due an All-Ireland in hurling every five years.

Waterford: The current crop of talented young hurlers has rekindled hope while also reminding many of the squandered noughties and the fallow decades before.

LEINSTER

Carlow: Chief sporting accomplishment in the last fifty years was producing Sean O'Brien.

Dublin: The masters of all they survey.

Kildare: Benny Coulter's square ball in 2010, the fruitless Micko years, an endless litany of drubbings at the hands of Dublin …

Kilkenny: Brian Cody could melt down his All-Ireland medals, cash in the gold, and become the richest man in Ireland overnight.

Laois: Chief sporting success story since 2003 is the broadcasting career of Colm Parkinson. Says it all really.

Longford: They haven't even had cause to be patronised in years, a sign of their irrelevance in the GAA's big picture.

Louth: Cursed/patronised. Joe Sheridan's goal in 2010 seemed like the act of a cruel god, but the patronising of the Wee County that followed was equally unseemly.

Meath: Two All-Ireland wins in the 1990s help people forget how mediocre the Royalers have been this century.

Offaly: Sated by semi-recent glories/patronised. Offaly's hurling wins in the 1990s prevent all-out despair. No All-Ireland winning team has been patronised more than the 1982 boys.

Westmeath: 2004 was fun and all, but there was little before it or after it to cling to.

Wexford: 1996 remains the pinnacle for all Wexford people. It's not that long ago, really.

Wicklow: Wicklow remains that county that everyone fears in the first round of the qualifiers but beats easily anyway.

ULSTER

Antrim: Haven't reach an All-Ireland final since 1989.

Armagh: Their 2002 team had more fascinating characters per capita than any other All-Ireland winning team.

Cavan: Patronised/cursed. Unfortunately those All-Ireland wins in the 1940s don't exactly count as semi-recent glories.

Derry: 1993 was a good while ago, but with Joe Brolly as the GAA's leading advocate of the spirit of the game, Derry can be proud of its contribution.

Donegal: More content than arrogant. The McGuinness years were ones of impossible dreaming.

Down: Five All-Ireland wins, including two in the 1990s, and the feeling of moral supremacy for playing inherently pretty football.

Fermanagh: Though various breakthroughs in the early noughties had supporters dying their sheep green (see page 52), they've never even won Ulster.

Monaghan: The media love to see the Farney Army on a high, mostly because they like saying the words 'Farney Army'. Decent in Clones, less so in Croker.

Tyrone: The glory days may be over, but those three All-Irelands in six years won't be forgotten for a long time. They were the team of the noughties.

2016 Sports Bucket List

2016 is gonna to be a massive year for sport: The Euros. Rio Olympics. It's going to be brilliant. Here are just a few of the sporting events we're saving our pennies for ...

FEB 7	Ireland v Wales, Six Nations, Aviva Stadium
FEB 8	Super Bowl 50, Levi's Stadium, Santa Clara, California
FEB 13	France v Ireland, Six Nations, Stade de France
FEB 27	England v Ireland, Six Nations, Twickenham
MARCH 12	Ireland v Italy, Six Nations, Aviva Stadium
MARCH 15–18	Cheltenham
MARCH 19	Ireland v Scotland, Six Nations, Aviva Stadium
MAY 14	Champions Cup final, Stade des Lumières, Lyon
MAY 28	Champions League final, San Siro
JUNE 10	Euro 2016 curtain-raiser, Saint-Denis
JULY 10	Euro 2016 final, Saint-Denis
AUG 5	Rio Olympics Opening Ceremony, the Maracanã
AUG 6	Boxing begins at Riocentro
AUG 14	100 metres final, Rio Olympics, Maracanã
SEPT 3	Aer Lingus Classic: Boston College vs Georgia Tech, Aviva Stadium
SEPT 4	All-Ireland hurling final, Croke Park
SEPT 18	All Ireland footbal final, Croke Park
SEPT 30–OCT 2	Ryder Cup, Hazeltine, Minnesota
DEC 26	Boxing Day Premier League fixtures

Crossword

ACROSS

3 Steve Staunton's affectionate nickname for Scottish opponents
5 Team Munster beat to win their first Heineken Cup
9 What do you think of that, _____ ____?
10 Nearly killed BOD in first 2005 Lions test
11 Welsh Rugby player involved in highway golf cart incident
12 Blew up the 1998 Clare-Offaly semifinal replay
13 First name of Giovanni Trappatoni's translator
15 Pooped on himself in Italia '90 match against Ireland
16 Most capped Irish frontrow

Answers on p.124.

DOWN

1 Tipp hurler with the best nickname in the GAA
2 This Irish international nearly lost his manhood to the goalposts for Liverpool in 1998
4 Ireland's greatest Olympian, counting only medals
6 Fear Munster more than Ireland
7 Coached Ireland before Big Jack
8 Month that Ireland traditionally plays its best football
9 Athenry hurler who went viral for wild man stuff in 2012 _____ Maher
10 Number of goals Ireland scored at Euro 2012 (en español)
11 This Wallace nearly cost Ireland the 2009 Grand Slam with late penalty
14 Scored winner for Holland against Ireland in Euro '88

Eamon Dunphy: Fact or Fiction?

Eamon Dunphy is a crank and a national treasure. How well do you know his life and his most famous sayings? Answers on p.124.

DID HE SAY IT?

1. '[Steven] Gerrard. Found out tonight. Nothing player.'
TRUE / FALSE

2. 'Kids these days have personal stereos and computers. They're not going out and playing football like they used to.' TRUE / FALSE

3. 'I believe the appointment of John Delaney as head of the FAI is a positive development for football in this country.'
TRUE / FALSE

4. 'I actually think that both Gerry Adams and Martin McGuinness are greater men than Michael Collins.' TRUE / FALSE

5. 'Mick McCarthy is a boil on the arse of Irish soccer.' TRUE / FALSE

6. 'England was the promised land. Trying to get away from this corrupt, priest-ridden kip of a place created out of the warped mind of Éamon de Valera was all we hoped for as kids.' TRUE / FALSE

7. 'That performance [against Egypt] would make you ashamed to be Irish.' TRUE / FALSE

8. 'I had these rural GAA men, who wouldn't know a football from a bag of cement, coming up to me telling me I was wrong about David O'Leary.' [On the Italia '90 period] TRUE / FALSE

9. 'We're talking trophies now, Jack.' [On Irish football in the late 1980s] TRUE / FALSE

10. '[Harry Kewell] is fat and a clown, Bill. A fat clown for all to see.'
TRUE / FALSE

11. '[Seamus Heaney] is a sham national poet deserving of real begrudgery.' TRUE / FALSE

12. 'Carragher would be better tying a wheelie bin to a bit of rope and trailing it around behind him.' [On the Jamie Carragher–Djimi Traoré partnership] TRUE / FALSE

13. 'You can't get good coke in this town.' TRUE / FALSE

14. [On the FAI taking €5 million from Blatter and FIFA after the Henry handball]: 'This is a bit of whatever you call it ... It's harmless ... I don't think it will do us reputational damage for the intelligent observer ... But not everyone is an intelligent observer.' TRUE / FALSE

DID HE DO IT?

15. Went on a date with Mary Robinson in 1968. TRUE / FALSE

16. Accused John Giles of breaking his friend's leg. TRUE / FALSE

17. Was expelled from two different schools as a kid. TRUE / FALSE

18. Was a speechwriter for Fine Gael in the early 1980s. TRUE / FALSE

19. Wrote he would probably vote No in the divorce referendum. TRUE / FALSE

20. Wore a black armband while playing for Millwall the week after Bloody Sunday. TRUE / FALSE

21. Played Gaelic Football for St Joseph's/O'Connell Boys as a kid. TRUE / FALSE

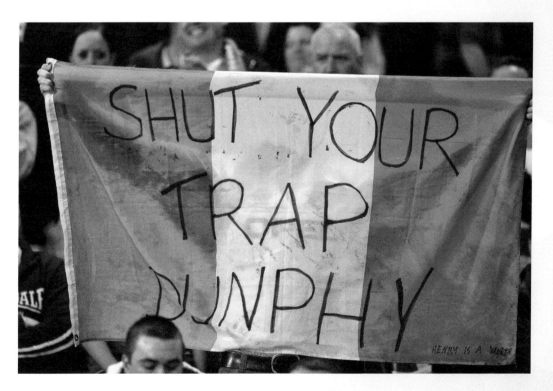

How Well Do You Know Dream Team?

We love *Dream Team*, you love *Dream Team*, everybody loves *Dream Team*! But now the time has come to prove your love. We at Balls.ie have compiled a rigorous quiz, with questions ranging from easy to impossible, for you to sink your teeth into. Do you know your Viv Wrights from your Jamie Parkers? Your Didier Baptistes from your Marcel Sabatiers? Answers on p.124.

1. Easy start: what was the name of Harchester United's home stadium?
A. The Dragon's Lair.
B. Deepdale.
C. The City of Harchester Stadium.
D. The Dell.

2. From which club did Harchester sign football icon Luis Amor Rodriguez?
A. Barcelona.
B. Real Betis.
C. Levante.
D. Boca Juniors.

3. Who did Harchester United beat in the FA Cup final before an assassination attempt on Luis Amor Rodriguez?
A. Newcastle.
B. Manchester United.
C. Arsenal.
D. Chelsea.

4. Why did Jason Porter get a start with Harchester United?
A. He found out the manager had slept with the chairman's wife and used it to blackmail them.
B. He abused the manager from the sidelines and claimed he could do better.
C. He scored a hat-trick for the reserves.
D. Karl Fletcher was killed.

5. Which of the following Harchester United players was an Irish international?
A. Curtis Alexander.
B. Billy O'Neill.
C. Danny Rawsthorne.
D. Clyde Connelly.

6. Which European city were Harchester United flying back from when their plane crashed, killing everyone on board?
A. Lisbon.
B. Marseille.
C. Amsterdam.
D. Munich.

7. But why wasn't Luis Amor Rodriguez on the plane?
A. He was in Spain for transfer talks with Real Madrid.
B. He missed the flight because he was saving a family from a house fire.
C. He was recovering in hospital from an unrelated attempt on his life.
D. He missed the flight because he was in bed with Lynda Block.

8. Tough one here: how many Premier League goals did Karl Fletcher score in his career?
A. 47.
B. 112.
C. 72.
D. 172.

9. How did Karl Fletcher die?
A. He crashed his car while drink-driving.
B. He died in the Millennium Stadium bus explosion.
C. He was shot by Harchester police after being framed for murder.
D. He was impaled on a dressing room peg by his manager.

10. What ended Luke Davenport's career, after he had signed for a record fee with Barcelona?
A. Poor vision.
B. A complete ACL tear.
C. Prison.
D. Poor vision.

11. Which of the following players did Lynda Block not have sex with?
A. Ray Wyatt.
B. Karl Fletcher.
C. Prashant Dattani.
D. Luis Amor Rodriguez.

12. Which of the following Harchester players did not die during the show's run?
A. Lee Presley.
B. Jamie Parker.
C. Casper Rose.
D. Monday Bandele.

13. Which company secured the contract to make Harchester United's kit after Le Coq Sportif's contract expired?
A. Valsport.
B. Macron.
C. Puma.
D. Carbrini.

14. Who started the fire that burned Harchester United's stadium to the ground?
A. Don Barker.
B. Ray Wyatt.
C. Danny Sullivan.
D. Darren Tyson.

15. What was Jamie Parker best known for?
A. His solitary England cap.
B. Holding the team hostage in the dressing room with a gun.
C. Biting an opponent's ear off.
D. Saving the penalty that kept Harchester United in the Premier League.

16. What was Jamie Parker's wife called?
A. Torri.
B. Trish.
C. Tina.
D. Tash.

17. Which Northern Ireland town is Connor McCarthy from?
A. Newry.
B. Dungannon.
C. Bangor.
D. Coleraine.

18. What could Harchester United manager Don Barker not be described as?
A. Terrorist.
B. Rapist.
C. Arsonist.
D. Murderer.

19. What was Vivian Wright's nickname?
A. Jaws.
B. Vicious.
C. Psycho.
D. Skipper.

20. What secret was Frank Stone desperate to keep covered up?
A. He was racist.
B. He was colour-blind.
C. He was broke.
D. He was bisexual.

21. How did the final series end?
A. The team bus exploded outside the Millennium Stadium.
B. The whole team died of food poisoning.
C. Harchester United qualified for the Champions League on the last day of the season.
D. With an unconfirmed Premier League win in a burning stadium.

Did
Joe Brolly
Really Say That?

Joe Brolly has taken the mantle from Eamon Dunphy as Ireland's most outspoken pundit. So outrageous are many of his statements that it's difficult to tell a real one from a false one any more. Examine these statements and spot the Brollyisms. Answers on p.124.

1. 'I think Mayo will win an All-Ireland, but not in my lifetime. They suffer from a western inferiority complex. Us grim northerners shook it off. But Mayo haven't, and until they learn how to be ruthless, they'll continue to crumble.' TRUE / FALSE

2. 'If Tyrone introduced puke football, then on Sunday in Croke Park, Kerry were the little girl from *The Exorcist* whose head revolves as she machine-guns the walls with a torrent of vomit.' TRUE / FALSE

3. 'I think the antipathy to Ulster football from these lads [Spillane and O'Rourke] comes from a deep-seated Treaty guilt. They haven't quite come to terms with abandoning us in 1922.' TRUE / FALSE

4. 'With the Sky deal coming along – hold on, let me finish – I think it is inevitable that within a few years, you will see Rupert Murdoch dictating the times of GAA matches. You will absolutely see that.' TRUE / FALSE

5. 'A fortnight ago, Colm O'Rourke criticised the GPA for their elitism and was subjected to a co-ordinated backlash that would have done the Israeli lobby proud.' TRUE / FALSE

6. 'Ballymena Fenians are like Protestants, and you can quote me on that.' TRUE / FALSE

7. 'I don't think the Dalai Lama would have the power to remain sanguine when faced with talk of managing a group of young Tyronemen. They're entirely a different breed.' TRUE / FALSE

8. 'When you look at a team like Galway, you're witnessing a team entirely unaccustomed with how to play modern football. They still think it's 1998 out there.

They probably go home whistling that song 'Bitter Sweet Symphony' from the Verve. You'll remember that, Pat.' TRUE / FALSE

9. 'I remember in Trinity staging a sit-in to stop the authorities carting a condom machine out of the student bar. It was our own Tiananmen Square.' TRUE / FALSE

10. 'All I ever wanted was to win an All-Ireland. You thought it was some type of Holy Grail, but in fact it was just a massive anti-climax. I remember waking up next morning and thinking, "What the fuck was all the fuss about?"' TRUE / FALSE

11. 'Newsflash: in wake of shock discovery that Sam Maguire was an IRB assassin, All-Ireland to be renamed "The Free State Press Corps Trophy".' TRUE / FALSE

12. 'Jim McGuinness is the Leonid Brezhnev of the GAA in many respects.' TRUE / FALSE

13. 'I find UFC to be an entirely distasteful sport at the centre of an insufferably commercial world that glamorises violence.' TRUE / FALSE

14. 'A friend of mine told me a story once about a drunken night in Dublin when she was a university student. She fell in with a student from Cavan and they ended up back in her place. After a bit of passionate kissing on the sofa, she suggested they move to the bedroom. Just as they were climbing into the bed, he suddenly stopped and said to her, "There's something I want to do." "What is it?" she said. He hesitated for a second, then blurted out, "Ah f*** it, I'm just going to do it." As she looked on in bemusement, he stood bolt upright and sang the whole of Amhrán na bhFiann at the top of his voice. At the height of his passion, that was what came into his mind.'
TRUE / FALSE

John Delaney
Word Scramble

There is no character in Irish sport – or indeed Irish life – quite like FAI chief executive John Delaney. No doubt some day his accumulated adventures will fill an unendingly long tome by Barry Egan. Until then, we have this word scramble. The clues below each correspond to a memorable episode of Delaney's tenure as FAI boss. Unscramble the answer to prove your John Delaney knowledge. Answers on p.124.

CLUES:

1. Was filmed singing this rebel song after Ireland beat USA in November 2014.
2. Described the time when his shoes were allegedly stolen by Irish supporters in this Polish resort town as 'a bit of folklore'.
3. Organised this for Irish supporters after game with Slovakia was moved in 2010.
4. Gave this form of neckwear to Irish supporters after draw with Russia in Moscow.
5. Negotiated this sum for payback from FIFA after the Thierry Henry handball.
6. Henry Winter of the *Telegraph* described said payment as this.
7. Is the pride of this county.
8. Famously earns more than this man.
9. Girlfriend Emma English described him as this in the *Sindo*.
10. Common refrain of people who want change in Irish football.

SCRAMBLED KEY:

1. NCN JLLEDOOEM   _ _ _ _ _ _ _ _ _ _
2. OOSPT   _ _ _ _ _
3. OSTNI CRIDA   _ _ _ _ _ _ _ _ _ _
4. ITE   _ _ _
5. EFMI INOIVLL   _ _ _ _ _ _ _ _ _ _ _
6. MYOOO NDEBL   _ _ _ _ _ _ _ _ _ _
7. RADFWTREO   _ _ _ _ _ _ _ _ _
8. BAAOM   _ _ _ _ _
9. FDR TIDYG EBBA   _ _ _ _ _ _ _ _ _ _ _ _
10. YNDUAEL OET   _ _ _ _ _ _ _ _ _

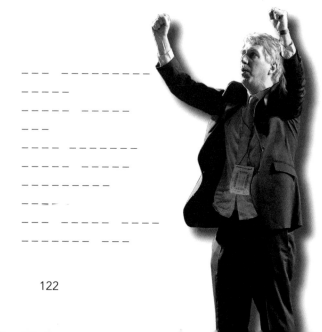

Wordsearch:
Terry Phelan's
Club Career

Legend of USA '94 and the first man to celebrate
with Ray Houghton after he scored against Italy,
Terry Phelan is beloved by Irish football supporters.
But can you identify the clubs that employed
Phelan on a full-time basis over a storied twenty-
five-year career that took him from England
to New Zealand to the little-known American
Soccer League? There are ten answers. They run
horizontally and vertically.

```
A  U  C  H  A  R  L  E  S  T  O  N
J  Z  E  V  E  R  T  O  N  P  L  Y
T  R  Z  I  C  G  G  K  W  V  Z  F
I  B  L  W  I  M  B  L  E  D  O  N
V  J  E  A  L  M  S  O  X  Q  L  W
J  X  E  F  U  L  H  A  M  K  Z  H
U  A  D  S  W  A  N  S  E  A  E  E
C  X  S  I  R  O  T  A  G  O  P  C
S  H  E  F  F  I  E  L  D  U  T  D
C  H  E  L  S  E  A  W  Y  C  Z  K
R  O  V  U  Y  A  K  N  P  X  A  N
S  M  A  N  C  I  T  Y  J  M  E  H
```

Fun Pages
Answers

Crossword, p.113:

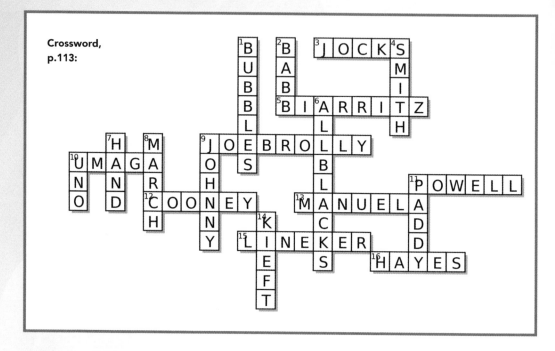

Across / Down solution letters:

- JOCKS
- SMITH
- BIARRITZ
- JOE BROLLY
- UMAGA
- POWELL
- COONEY
- MANUELA
- LINEKER
- HAYES
- BUBBLE
- BABBLE
- JOHNNY
- MHAND
- MARRYH
- NONO
- KIEFT
- LEFT
- ALBLACKADDS

Eamon Dunphy quiz, p.116: 1. True. 2. False. 3. True. 4. True. 5. False. 6. False. 7. False. 8. False. 9. True. 10. True. 11. True. 12. True. 13. True. 14. True. 15. False. 16. True. 17. False. 18. True. 19. True. 20. True. 21. False.

Dream Team quiz, p.118: 1. A. 2. B. 3. B. 4. B. 5. C. 6. C. 7. A. 8. D. 9. D. 10. A. 11. C. 12. D. 13. A. 14. C. 15. B. 16. D. 17. A. 18. C. 19. A. 20. D. 21. D.

Joe Brolly quiz, p.120: 1. False. 2. True. 3. False. 4. False. 5. True. 6. True. 7. False. 8. False. 9. False. 10. True. 11. True. 12. False. 13. False. 14. True.

John Delaney, p.122:

1. JOE MCDONNELL
2. SOPOT
3. DISCO TRAIN
4. TIE
5. FIVE MILLION
6. BLOOD MONEY
7. WATERFORD
8. OBAMA
9. BIG TEDDY BEAR
10. DELANEY OUT

Terry Phelan, p.123 (see right):

CHARLESTON
CHELSEA
EVERTON
FULHAM
LEEDS
MAN CITY
OTAGO
SHEFFIELD UTD
SWANSEA
WIMBLEDON

```
A  U  C  H  A  R  L  E  S  T  O  N
J  Z  E  V  E  R  T  O  N  P  L  Y
T  R  Z  I  C  G  G  K  W  V  Z  F
I  B  L  W  I  M  B  L  E  D  O  N
V  J  E  A  L  M  S  O  X  Q  L  W
J  X  E  F  U  L  H  A  M  K  Z  H
U  A  D  S  W  A  N  S  E  A  E  H
C  X  S  I  R  O  T  A  G  O  P  C
S  H  E  F  F  I  E  L  D  U  T  D
C  H  E  L  S  E  A  W  Y  C  Z  K
R  O  V  U  Y  A  K  N  P  X  A  N
S  M  A  N  C  I  T  Y  J  M  E  H
```

A NOTE ON PHOTOGRAPHY

The Balls.ie Guide To Life features the outstanding work of Ireland's premier sports photography agency, Sportsfile. For more than thirty years, Sportsfile has been documenting every important event in Irish sporting life.

This book includes photographs by David Aliaga, Daire Brennan, Matt Browne, Ramsey Cardy, Damien Eagers, Cody Glenn, Diarmuid Greene, Brian Lawless, Lukasz Grochala, Ray Lohan, Jerry Kennelly, David Maher, Stephen McCarthy, Ray McManus, Oliver McVeigh, Paul Mohan, Brendan Moran, Pat Murphy, Piaras Ó Midheach, Aoife Rice & Ray Ryan.

Thanks to Ray McManus and everyone in Sportsfile for their help in the production of this book. Find out more at www.sportsfile.com.

ACKNOWLEDGEMENTS

The Balls.ie team would like to thank all of its readers for their loyalty and devotion to the site down through the years. Thanks to Barry Downes for the illustrations, and to Nicola Reddy, Emma Byrne and Michael O'Brien from The O'Brien Press for their assistance with the production of *The Balls.ie Guide to Life.*